GLUTEN FREE COOKBOOK

1200 Days of Easy & Flavorful Recipes to Delight Your Taste Buds and Embark on a Savory and Affordable Gluten-Free Adventure

Luna Edwards

Copyright © 2023 by Luna Edwards - All rights reserved.

No part of this publication may be reproduced, distributed, or transmitted in any form or by any means, including photocopying, recording, or other electronic or mechanical methods, without the prior written permission of the publisher, except in the case of brief quotations embodied in critical reviews and certain other noncommercial uses permitted by copyright law.

This book is designed to provide information about the subject matter covered. It is sold with the understanding that the author are not engaged in rendering medical, health, psychological, or any other kind of personal professional services. If expert assistance or counseling is needed, the services of a competent professional should be sought.

The author specifically disclaim any liability, loss, or risk that is incurred as a consequence, directly or indirectly, of the use and application of any of the contents of this book.

CONTENTS

INTRODUCTION — 5
Undesrtanding gluten — 7
Gluten-free ingredients — 8
The Art of Substitutions — 10
The Perfect Pizza — 13
Managing the Diet — 14
Smart Savings — 17

BREAKFAST — 20

LUNCH — 33

DINNER — 49

SNACK & APPETIZERS — 65

DESSERT — 78

BREAD, PASTA & PIZZA — 94

CONCLUSION — 106

Appendix — 107

INTRODUCTION

Welcome to the world of gluten-free cooking, a place where incredible flavor meets unbeatable nutrition and unrivaled delight. As someone who's chosen or had to adopt this special diet, I'm here to assure you that you're definitely not alone in your journey!

My own path towards living a life free from gluten began when I was diagnosed with an intolerance for it - something which at first felt like an insurmountable challenge. But now? Now my mission is to prove that going without wheat doesn't mean sacrificing taste or variety; it simply means opening up an entire new realm of flavours and textures waiting to be explored! And so, this cookbook is the result of trial and error experiments resulting in delicious recipes full of health benefits.

It's time to take your gluten-free journey to the next level! In this book, you'll find clear and concise information about celiac disease, gluten sensitivity and all things related to going gluten-free. We've got a plethora of delicious recipes for every occasion, from quick weeknight meals to extravagant holiday feasts. Plus, we provide practical tips on how to make GF eating less expensive and easier for everyone in the family so that it can be an enjoyable experience rather than a chore.

But more importantly, we want this book not just as culinary source but also as an inspiration tool: no matter what obstacles life throws at you—be it cooking without wheat or anything else—it is still possible with enough dedication and resourcefulness. So don't shy away from exploring new flavors; wear your metaphorical apron proudly; let's embark on this flavorful journey together! Bon appétit!

UNDERSTANDING GLUTEN

Gluten is a word that's been thrown around a lot lately, but what does it really mean? Well, gluten is basically just a mixture of proteins found in grains like wheat, rye and barley. It's actually the reason why breads are so chewy and yummy - it gives dough its elasticity which allows bread to rise during baking. But unfortunately for some of us out there with celiac disease, consuming even small amounts of gluten can be incredibly damaging.

Celiac disease is an autoimmune disorder where ingesting gluten causes damage to the small intestine which interferes with nutrient absorption from food leading to malnutrition or even worse; osteoporosis and intestinal cancer in rare cases. Symptoms vary wildly between individuals: diarrhea, bloating or abdominal pain are classic indicators but others might suffer fatigue or depression without any visible physical signs at all - making diagnosis notoriously difficult! In fact it's almost as hard as finding Waldo on one those Where's Wally books you used have when you were younger (trust me I know!).

If you think your body isn't reacting well after eating something containing gluten then please see your doctor right away because everyone deserves good health no matter who they are!

It's essential to understand that celiac disease and non-celiac gluten sensitivity are two distinct medical conditions. If you think you suffer from either, it is highly recommended that you consult a healthcare professional right away for proper diagnosis. Contrary to popular belief, a gluten-free diet isn't just some trendy fad or miracle cure for weight loss – it's a necessary treatment option for those who have celiac disease or non-celiac gluten sensitivity as avoiding gluten is the only way to maintain gut health and prevent symptoms from occurring. Interestingly, individuals with non-celiac gluten sensitivity can experience similar symptoms of celiac disease after consuming wheat products but without any intestinal damage which makes diagnosing this condition even more challenging!

Living gluten-free can seem like a challenge, but it doesn't have to be. It's all about learning how to navigate the grocery store and cook with new ingredients. To really get the hang of it, you need to read food labels carefully so that hidden sources of gluten don't sneak into your meals - think sauces, dressings and additives. But there is an upside! You'll soon discover tasty alternatives such as quinoa flour or almond meal for baking delicious cakes and treats without any traces of wheat-based products.

In the next chapter, we'll explore gluten-free ingredients in more detail and how they can be used to create delicious dishes.

GLUTEN-FREE INGREDIENTS

Imagining walking through a doorway to a land of endless culinary possibilities can be daunting, but it's time to take the plunge into gluten-free cooking! From flavorful flours to exciting ingredients that bring your dishes alive, this chapter will show you all there is to explore.

Flours

At the center of it all is gluten-free flour: an incredibly versatile tool with its own unique characteristics depending on what type you choose. There are so many options available these days that even those just starting out in their GF journey won't be at a loss for choice or flavor!

Rice Flour: Nothing says "gluten-free" like rice flour. This baking staple is made by grinding either white or brown rice into a delicately flavored, light powder that's perfect for whipping up cakes and pastries. I still remember my first attempt at making Thanksgiving cookies with this stuff - the crumbly texture was a hit!

Corn Flour: Corn flour or polenta has been gaining attention lately as another gluten-free option. It's produced from milled corn kernels which adds an earthier flavor to dishes than rice flour does. Try using it in muffins, breads, and even crepes for some added color and crunch! My friend from the Midwest taught me how to make her special cornbread recipe - it'll quickly become your go-to comfort food dish if you haven't tried it already!

Buckwheat Flour: Buckwheat isn't wheat but don't let the name fool you; this hearty grain is just as versatile when ground into a fine powder. Its nutty taste pairs perfectly with pancake batter so why not try adding buckwheat pancakes to your breakfast rotation? The smell of these delicious flapjacks takes me back all those years ago when I used to help my mom make them on chilly winter mornings – delicious memories every time!

Teff Flour: native to Ethiopia and full of protein, fiber, and iron - it has a sweet nutty flavor that's perfect for baking breads, cakes or cookies.

Amaranth Flour: is another ancient grain with an interesting history – the Aztecs & Maya treasured it highly! Slightly peppery in taste; this gluten-free ingredient can be used for baking muffins or cookies too.

Tapioca Flour: comes from the cassava root & makes a wonderful thickener for sauces as well as soups & desserts. It has an incredibly light texture and neutral flavor which makes it so versatile in cooking!

Other Gluten-Free Flours: There are many other gluten-free flours to explore, like almond flour, quinoa flour, and coconut flour. I discovered coconut flour during a trip to Hawaii and it has since become a staple ingredient in my summer recipes.

Other Ingredients
Besides flours, there are plenty of delicious and creative gluten-free ingredients to use in your cooking.

Cornstarch: is an amazing thickener for soups and sauces; plus it can be used as a breading when frying chicken - giving you that perfectly crunchy crust!

Potato starch: adds a light texture to baked goods but can be used for savory dishes too like gnocchi – talk about restaurant quality right in the comfort of home! Is particularly useful for thickening sauces and soups, and can also be used to make light and fluffy desserts.

Gluten-Free Yeast: There are several alternatives to gluten-containing yeast, such as gluten-free brewer's yeast and sourdough. Gluten-free brewer's yeast can be used for breads and other leavened treats, while sourdough might require a bit more effort but will give your goodies an amazing texture and unbeatable flavor. When we were stuck indoors during the pandemic, I decided to take on this challenge myself - it was definitely difficult at times, but so worth it in the end!

Basic Gluten-Free ingredients: basic ingredients like eggs, gluten-free milk and vegetable oil can help us create some mouthwatering dishes! Eggs are a go-to ingredient for many people on a gluten-free diet; they help bind together different elements while also providing a soft texture to baked goods. Almond or rice milk is an excellent substitution for regular dairy if you're trying to keep things as GF as possible. And let's not forget about good ol' vegetable oil -it's so versatile and perfect whether you're frying something up or adding it into salads for extra zestiness (shout out to my vegan homie who showed me the power of coconut oil!).

Gluten-free cooking isn't just about having dietary restrictions – it's also your chance to get creative with flavors and textures! Don't be afraid to experiment with these core ingredients: who knows what kind of culinary masterpiece you'll come up with? Let your imagination run wild...you got this!

THE ART OF SUBSTITUTIONS

In this chapter, we will delve into the heart of gluten-free cooking: substitutions. Yes, you heard right! You don't have to give up your favorite dishes just because they contain gluten. There are many gluten-free alternatives that can replace traditional ingredients. But how do you know which ingredients to use and in what quantities? Don't worry, we are here to guide you on this journey.

Common Substitutions

Wheat Flour: don't worry if your favorite dishes are off limits because they contain wheat flour - there's an abundance of alternatives out there! From rice flour and almond flour to coconut flour and cornflour, each one brings its own flavor and texture profile for you to experiment with until you find the perfect match for your recipe. Just remember that these flours tend to absorb more liquid than regular wheat so make sure to adjust accordingly - start by adding 1.25 times the amount of GF flour called for in any given recipe and go from there!

Bread: gone are the days of limiting your bread and pasta choices due to dietary restrictions! You can now find plenty of delicious gluten-free options in stores or even make it at home. For homemade gluten-free bread, you'll need a mix of GF flours like the ones mentioned above; plus leavening agents such as yeast or baking powder - and don't forget xanthan gum or psyllium for that classic elastic texture we all know and love. To get started on this recipe transformation game: think 1 cup flour : 1 teaspoon xanthan gum/psyllium :1 teaspoon yeast for every cup wheat flour from your original dish.

Pasta: pasta is also getting an upgrade with alternatives like rice pasta, corn pasta & lentil noodles - each offering unique textures & flavors that will take any dinner night up a notch (or two). And when needing to switch out wheat based pastas you won't have to do too much math – just remember the magic ratio here is always one-for-one! Be mindful though since these bad boys cook faster than their traditional counterparts so keep an eye on them while they're boiling away lest you want overcooked mush instead of al dente perfection.

Pizza: pizza is one of the most beloved dishes around, but unfortunately it usually contains gluten in its base. But don't worry - if you're looking for a delicious and safe alternative, there are tons to choose from! A great way to make your own pizza at home is by using a mix of gluten-free flours like rice flour, almond flour or quinoa flour as the base. Alternatively, you can buy pre-made bases that are already certified gluten-free. As far as sauces go, many brands offer ready-to-use options which should all be checked before use – just to make sure they don't contain any hidden surprises! When it comes to toppings there's an abundance of choice; think meats like chicken or bacon strips combined with fresh vegetables such as peppers and mushrooms – whatever takes your fancy! Just remember not to add anything containing hidden sources of gluten (such as some sausages). When baking up your masterpiece in the oven keep this top tip in mind: Pre bake the crust for around 5 minutes so that when adding on those yummy sauces and toppings it won't become too soggy leading to a broken crusty mess. Since traditional wheat flour has less density than GF alternatives you might need lower temperatures and longer cooking times - no one wants undercooked dough after all!

Sauces and Dressings: there are plenty of options for sauces and dressings that won't trigger any sensitivities or allergies! Instead of regular soy sauce, reach for the gluten free variety like tamari - it's naturally made without wheat flour so you don't have to worry about cross contamination. If you're looking for something creamy and delicious to top your meal off with, cornstarch or rice flour can be used as an alternative thickener instead of wheat flour. Having these ingredients on hand in your pantry ensures that creating a tasty and safe dish doesn't require much effort at all!

Beer: when it comes to beer, it can be a tricky one when trying to stay gluten-free. Thankfully, there are plenty of options on the market that use barley or other grains without gluten. If you're looking for an easier option, cider is always naturally free from anything containing gluten - so that's your go-to! Just keep in mind though, if something is labeled as 'low-gluten' doesn't mean it's actually completely free from any trace elements of the protein - so make sure you read those labels carefully and double check everything before taking your first sip!

Breakfast Cereals: many breakfast cereals contain gluten, but there are many gluten-free alternatives. You can opt for corn flakes or rice flakes, or cereals based on quinoa. Just make sure to check the label to confirm they are gluten-free.

Top 10 Secrets to Adapting Your Recipes

The best tricks and tips for transforming your favorite recipes into delicious gluten-free dishes. Get ready to discover new flavors and techniques that will allow you to enjoy your favorite dishes without worrying about gluten.

1. **Experiment with different flours:** Rice flour is light and neutral while almond flour has an intense flavor and texture - so pick whichever one suits your recipe best.

2. **Adjust the amounts of liquids:** gluten-free flours absorb more than wheat ones so add some extra if it looks a bit dry.

3. **Don't forget binding agents:** are essential in creating that elastic texture we know all too well from regular recipes. Psyllium in particular, not only helps to give elasticity to baked goods, but also adds extra fiber, making your dishes more filling. Try adding a teaspoon of xanthan gum or psyllium for every cup of gluten-free flour.

4. **Check the cooking:** To ensure delicious results, keep a close eye on the oven and check regularly. Gluten free baked goods are known to cook faster than their regular counterparts.

5. **Cover to maintain moisture:** Gluten-free baked goods tend to dry out more easily. A simple trick to maintain moisture is to cover your dish with aluminum foil during cooking.

6. **Experiment and have fun:** The key to adapting recipes is experimentation. Don't be afraid to try new things and make mistakes. In the end, that's how you learn and grow as cooks. And remember, we're here to help you at every step of your gluten-free journey.

7. **Use a mix of flours:** Mixing up different gluten-free flours can bring a delicious complexity of flavor and texture that's reminiscent of wheat flour. Here are some tasty combinations to inspire your baking:

- Rice flour, potato flour, and tapioca flour mix: This mix is light and neutral, making it suitable for most baking recipes, like cakes, cookies, and bread.
- Almond flour, coconut flour, and tapioca flour mix: This mix has a richer flavor and a heavier texture, making it suitable for desserts like cakes and muffins.
- Buckwheat flour, rice flour, and amaranth flour mix: This mix has an earthy flavor and a robust texture, making it suitable for savory baked goods like bread and focaccia.
- Quinoa flour, rice flour, and potato flour mix: This mix has a unique flavor and a light texture, making it suitable for baked goods like muffins and pancakes.
- Bean flour, rice flour, and corn flour mix: This mix has a rich flavor and a heavy texture, making it suitable for savory baked goods like bread and tortillas.
-

Remember, these are just suggestions and you may need to get creative in order to concoct the perfect blend for your recipe. The amount of each flour used can depend on what you're working with, so don't be discouraged if it takes a few tries before reaching your desired consistency and flavor.

8. **Add proteins:** Some gluten-free flours, like bean flour or lentil flour, can add extra protein to your dishes, making them more filling. These flours also have a richer flavor and can add depth to your recipes.

9. **Experiment with cooking techniques:** gluten-free recipes don't always have to follow the same cooking techniques as their wheat counterparts! You might find that your cookies turn out better at lower temperatures or that moist environments help bread rise properly - so go ahead and experiment with different methods until you get something truly delectable!

10. **Don't forget about flavor:** It's essential to focus on texture and structure when making gluten-free dishes, but don't forget the flavor! Adding herbs, extracts, spices or other seasonings can take your meal from good to great. It's important that you put as much thought into the taste of your creation as its physical form.

We hope these additional tricks help you perfect your skills in gluten-free cooking and create dishes that you and your loved ones will adore.

THE PERFECT PIZZA

Pizza is a beloved dish by all, but why not take it up a notch and make gluten-free pizza that's just as delicious? Crafting the perfect gluten-free pizza dough can be intimidating but with some savvy tips you'll have yourself a crisp and scrumptious pizza to wow everyone. Here are some actionable guidelines for constructing the ideal gluten-free pizza crust.

1. The flour matter: Not all GF flours will give you excellent results so try blending together brown rice flour, sorghum flour, and potato starch for an optimal texture with no overpowering taste.

2. Don't forget the xanthan gum: This food additive serves as your secret weapon in place of traditional wheat gluten - about 1 teaspoon per cup of GF flour should do the trick!

3. Water is key: Gluten-free ingredients tend to absorb more water than those containing regular wheat so add extra H20 until your dough feels moist without getting too sticky!

4. Resting time: After mixing together all those gf components, give them some well deserved downtime by allowing your doughy creation to chillax for no less than thirty minutes – this allows everything enough time for absorption which will ultimately improve consistency. You could even extend this relaxing period over several hours (or even leave it overnight) if you really wanted those extra flavours!

5. Roll out carefully: delicately roll out said dough with experienced hands or flour coated rolling pins – don't attempt perfection here as sometimes these 'rustic' pizzas are just so darn charming!

6. Pre-baking is your friend: Before adding the topping, bake the dough in the oven for 5-7 minutes at 420°F. This helps to create a crispy crust and prevents the dough from becoming too moist when you add the ingredients. Using a pizza stone can further help achieve this. If you don't have a pizza stone, you can preheat a baking sheet in the oven before adding the dough.

7. Experiment with toppings: Don't be afraid to get creative with your pizza toppings! Why not try a gluten-free pesto pizza topped with buffalo mozzarella and juicy cherry tomatoes? Or, go for something sweet like a chocolate cream base and fresh fruit - YUM!

8. The key here is practice: Don't give up if the first attempt doesn't quite hit the spot. With time, you'll find out what ingredients and techniques work best for you. So don't forget: have fun while experimenting in the kitchen!

MANAGING THE DIET

Living gluten-free isn't something that has to be endured alone--it can actually bring you and your family closer together. When I was first diagnosed with a gluten intolerance, it was initially confusing and worrisome for my loved ones. But then we realized this could be an opportunity to come together as a unit, become more aware of our diets, and thrive despite the challenge.

If someone in your household is living gluten free while others aren't, it's important to educate everyone on what it means and why it's necessary for their health. Understanding each other's needs goes a long way towards fostering harmony within the home! When I explained my condition to my family they were eager to help me manage my diet so that living gluten-free wouldn't feel like such an isolating experience.

By being open about dietary restrictions but also making sure there are still plenty of delicious meals suitable for everyone at the table, families can find ways of uniting around food instead of separating due too different eating habits or preferences - even if some members have special dietary requirements like myself!

Organizing the pantry and fridge can seem like a real chore, but with some strategic thinking it can be done in no time. Designate a "gluten-free corner" of your pantry for all the delicious gluten-free snacks and ingredients you find on your grocery runs. Utilize containers labeled to avoid cross contamination between gluten-containing foods and those without.

Creating family meal plans that cater to everyone's dietary needs will not only ensure everyone is getting what they need nutritionally, but also make dinner preparation much easier. Not every night has to be dedicated solely towards making something gluten free; however, having options available at each mealtime is important for those who do require it. For example, when I'm cooking up dinner for my family I usually whip up one main dish that's totally free of wheat products then just add sides according to preference - whether we're going GF or not!

A gluten-free diet isn't something to dread - it's an opportunity. As you adjust your routine and try out new foods and recipes, keep a positive attitude; each step counts! My diagnosis of gluten intolerance was not only liberating but also gave me the chance to rediscover my love for cooking. Now I'm able to whip up delicious meals that everyone in my family enjoys without compromising on health or taste.

It's important to set a good example for the rest of your family as well - by staying motivated and sticking with this lifestyle change you can encourage them too. Our life has been enriched since I went gluten-free; we communicate better, understand each other's needs more clearly, and even get creative together when experimenting with different dishes! We wouldn't trade this experience for anything else – so embrace it wholeheartedly and enjoy every moment of this journey!

Being gluten-free isn't always easy, which is why it's important to celebrate all the little wins along the journey. Whether you just found a new favorite biscuit or successfully whipped up a meal that everyone can enjoy - every step counts and should be celebrated! I remember when I finally baked my first successful loaf of gluten-free bread; although it wasn't perfect, we were so proud of ourselves for creating something from scratch and savored every bite like it was award winning.

Navigating life with dietary restrictions as part of your family may seem daunting but armed with determination, an open mind and plenty of support from those around you - success is within reach! So get ready to take on this challenge with enthusiasm knowing that in time, these moments will become not only manageable but also enjoyable for everyone involved.

Avoiding Cross-Contamination

When following a gluten-free diet, it's essential to be vigilant about the risk of cross-contamination with other foods that contain gluten. Even trace amounts of gluten can cause serious problems for those who are intolerant - so here are some simple steps you can take to prevent this from happening:

1. Get organized: clear out space in your kitchen specifically for storing and preparing gluten-free meals. Consider having separate shelves in the fridge, drawers in the pantry or even two different sets of utensils like knives, cutting boards and pots & pans. Toaster bags also come handy if there's only one available appliance. Make sure your work area is clean before you start cooking up any GF goodies.

2 Label it up!: always remember to store all GF items properly labelled as "Gluten Free". Not only will this help keep them separated from regular food but make sure nothing gets mixed up by accident either! Let everyone at home know just how important it is not mess around with labels otherwise they might end up eating something unexpected (and probably unwelcome).

3. Avoid surface contamination: clean work surfaces, utensils, and kitchen equipment carefully after handling any food that contains gluten. Make sure these items get washed with hot water and soap or run through the dishwasher if possible - it's crucial to remove every trace so you don't accidentally ingest anything containing gluten.

4. Be mindful of ingredients: read labels closely for ingredients that might contain traces of or have been contaminated by gluten. Even something like salad dressing can unknowingly contain small amounts of this protein! To play it extra safe opt for certified 'gluten free' products whenever available too.

5. Communicate with your family: remind them about the importance of avoiding cross contamination when preparing meals in order to keep you safe from accidental exposure. Explain the precautions they need to take when handling gluten-containing foods and how they can support you in your gluten-free diet. This way, everyone will be more aware and careful during meal preparation and kitchen management.

6. Avoid double-dipping: Avoid using the same frying oil, pasta cooking water, or utensils for gluten-free and gluten-containing foods. Even these small amounts of gluten can cause problems. Make sure you have separate tools and ingredients to avoid any risk of cross-contamination.

By following these precautions, you can minimize the risk of cross-contamination with gluten and enjoy a safe and healthy gluten-free diet. Always remember to be vigilant and communicate openly with your family members and others when it comes to your gluten-free diet.

SMART SAVINGS

With some smart planning and savvy shopping strategies, it's possible to follow a gluten-free lifestyle and save money at the same time. To get started on your budget-friendly journey, I'll give you some top tips as well as show you where to find all the best bargains. So if living life sans gluten doesn't have to mean emptying out your wallet either - let's get saving!

Savvy Saving Tips

1. Opt for cheaper gluten-free carbohydrates: We all know that variety is the spice of life, and this also applies to the grains in our diet. However, when it comes to saving money, it might be helpful to take a closer look at what we're putting in our shopping cart. Grains like corn, rice, and gluten-free oats are excellent options that are not only wallet-friendly but also provide a solid base for a range of delicious dishes. So, the next time you go shopping, why not give these cheaper grains a chance?

2. Choose naturally gluten-free foods: there's no need to overspend on processed or packaged foods when nature has already provided us with its own wholesome goodies. Fruits, vegetables, tofu, nuts + legumes (the list goes on!) are all naturally gluten-free and packed full of essential nutrients - plus they tend to cost less than their store-bought counterparts! So if you really want to get your bang for your buck then make sure these items find their way into your diet as often as possible?

3. Bake your own goods: When you're looking to save money and have complete control of your ingredients, baking is the way to go! With this book in hand, even novice bakers can whip up delicious treats - think gluten-free breads or cookies that are sure to impress. Plus, there's something incredibly satisfying about making something with your own two hands.

4. Freeze extra meals and snacks: When you prepare a recipe, why not double the portions and freeze the rest? This will save you time and money in the future. For example, if you're preparing a gluten-free lasagna, you could make an extra portion and freeze it for a future meal. This will save you the time of preparing another meal from scratch and give you something ready to eat when you don't have the time or energy to cook.

5. Buy in bulk: Many gluten-free foods, like quinoa and lentils, can be bought in bulk at a lower cost. This can be particularly helpful if you have a large family or if you regularly consume these foods. Also, many stores offer discounts for bulk purchases, so you could save even more!

6. Make gluten-free meals a family affair: Instead of preparing separate meals for family members who follow a gluten-free diet and those who don't, why not try creating delicious gluten-free meals that the whole family can enjoy?

This will not only save you time but could also help raise awareness among your loved ones about the gluten-free diet and its potential health benefits. For example, you could try making a gluten-free pizza with a variety of toppings that everyone can appreciate, or a rich and nutritious salad with an abundance of vegetables, lean proteins, and a tasty gluten-free dressing. For desserts, you could try making gluten-free brownies or a fresh fruit dessert that everyone can enjoy.

7.Shop Smarter: Before you dive into a shopping spree, make sure to plan out meals and create a grocery list accordingly. This will save you from buying items that may be unnecessary while also avoiding spending more than necessary for convenience. A great example would be if your goal is to bake gluten-free cake – ensure all the ingredients are on your checklist before heading out! Doing this can help prevent those impulse purchases and keep extra cash in your pocketbook.

8.Use mainstream food products that are also gluten-free: For example, there are many brands of cereals, chips, and crackers that offer gluten-free options at reasonable prices. This can be a great way to save money, especially if you have children who love these types of snacks. Also, many of these products are available in traditional supermarkets, which means you won't have to make a special trip to a specialty food store to find them.

9. Join Facebook groups dedicated to gluten-free: is an awesome way of staying in-the-know about new products, deals and discounts at local stores. Plus, it's a great way to connect with others who follow a similar lifestyle - you can even get advice from them on how best to manage your dietary needs.

10.Avoid food waste: to make sure you're getting bang for your buck when grocery shopping, take some time out each week to plan out meals using ingredients already stocked in your kitchen - this'll help avoid any unnecessary impulse buys while also ensuring nothing goes off or gets thrown away needlessly. If there are certain items that need using up soonest then use them as inspiration for recipes; if chicken has been sitting around for too long then why not whip up something tasty like a spicy thai green curry?

Hunting for Best Deals and Discount

1. Exclusive coupons from gluten-free brand sites: You know, many gluten-free companies are aware that we want a bit of a discount on their products from time to time. For instance, Enjoy Life has a coupon for $1.50 off two items on their site which can really add up over time if you shop regularly. Other popular companies like Udi's, Franz, Glutino, Van's Lance and Simple Mills usually have coupons available as well so be sure to browse around for offers that fit your budget.

2. Walmart's Great Value brand: this product line offers cheaper alternatives to many gluten-free products without compromising quality or taste.

3 Shop at ALDI for gluten-free bread and baking mixes: if baking is more your style then head on over to ALDI where they carry liveGfree; an economical line of GF goods that will surprise even the most discerning shopper with its variety and top notch ingredients!

4. Save with Blue Apron: is a fantastic option if you don't want to deal with all the hassle of prepping meals yourself but still want a wide variety of options (plus they have $30 off your first order!). Not only do they conveniently deliver directly to your home but they also allow customers to specify allergens so as not compromise anyone's dietary restrictions – talk about an A+ service!

5. Buy gluten-free products from Trader Joe's: Trader Joe's has a fantastic selection of gluten-free products at reasonable prices. Take a look at their selection the next time you go shopping.

6. Buy in bulk from Costco: Buying in large quantities can be a great way to save on gluten-free foods. Costco has a wide selection of gluten-free products, so it might be worth a visit if you have one nearby.

Overall, there are many options to save on gluten-free products. Whether you choose to search for online coupons, shop at specific brands, or buy in bulk, the important thing is that you don't have to compromise your health or well-being to save money. So, the next time you find yourself grocery shopping, remember these tips. You might be surprised at how much you can save!

Breakfast

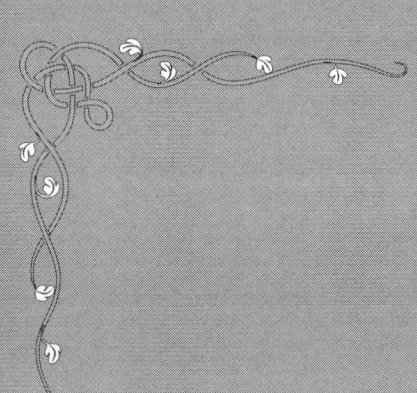

OAT PANCAKES WITH BLUEBERRIES

Prep time:
10 minutes

Cooking Time:
15 minutes

Servings:
4

INGREDIENTS:

- 2 cups of gluten-free oats (easily available in grocery stores)
- 1 cup of almond milk
- 2 large eggs
- 1 teaspoon of vanilla extract
- 2 tablespoons of honey
- 1 teaspoon of baking powder
- 1 cup of fresh blueberries

DIRECTIONS:

1. In a blender, combine the oats, almond milk, eggs, vanilla extract, honey, and baking powder. Blend until you get a smooth mixture.
2. Heat a non-stick pan over medium heat. Pour a ladle of batter for each pancake.
3. Add some blueberries on the surface of each pancake.
4. Cook for 2-3 minutes per side, or until they are golden.
5. Serve hot with fresh blueberries and extra honey if desired.

NUTRITIONS:

Calories: 220, Fat: 5g, Carbohydrates: 35g, Protein: 10g, Fiber: 5g, Sugars: 10g

TIPS:

If you don't have any fresh blueberries, frozen ones work just as well! Just make sure to thaw them out before adding them to your recipe.

SPINACH AND FETA FRITTATA

 **Prep time:** 15 minutes

 **Cooking Time:** 20 minutes

 **Servings:** 4

INGREDIENTS:

- 8 large eggs
- 1/2 cup of milk
- 1 cup of fresh spinach
- 1/2 cup of crumbled feta
- Salt and pepper to taste

DIRECTIONS:

1. Preheat the oven to 375°F (190°C).
2. In a medium bowl, beat the eggs with the milk. Add the spinach, feta, salt, and pepper.
3. Pour the mixture into a baking dish lined with parchment paper.
4. Bake for 20 minutes, or until the frittata is golden and cooked.
5. Let it cool for a few minutes before cutting and serving.

NUTRITIONS:

Calories: 250, Fat: 18g, Carbohydrates: 3g, Protein: 20g, Fiber: 1g, Sugars: 2g

TIPS:

If you prefer, swap the feta for a gluten-free cheese of your choice if that's something that better fits with your dietary needs.

BANANA AND STRAWBERRY SMOOTHIE

 **Prep time:** 5 minutes	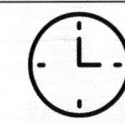 **Cooking Time:** 00 minutes	 **Servings:** 2

INGREDIENTS:

- 2 ripe bananas
- 1 cup of fresh strawberries
- 1 cup of almond milk
- 1 tablespoon of honey (optional)

DIRECTIONS:

1. In a blender, add the bananas, strawberries, almond milk, and honey.
2. Blend until you get a smooth and creamy mixture.
3. Pour into two glasses and serve immediately.

NUTRITIONS:

Calories: 150, Fat: 1g, Carbohydrates: 36g, Protein: 2g, Fiber: 5g, Sugars: 21g

TIPS:

why not add some chia seeds or flaxseeds in there for an extra boost of fiber and omega-3 fatty acids?

QUINOA AND APPLE PORRIDGE

Prep time:
5 minutes

Cooking Time:
15 minutes

Servings:
2

INGREDIENTS:

- 1 cup of quinoa
- 2 cups of water
- 1 large apple, diced
- 1 teaspoon of cinnamon
- 2 tablespoons of maple syrup

DIRECTIONS:

1. In a pot, bring the water to a boil. Add the quinoa, reduce the heat, cover, and let it cook for 15 minutes.
2. Once the quinoa is cooked, add the apple, cinnamon, and maple syrup. Stir well.
3. Divide the porridge into two bowls and serve hot.

NUTRITIONS:

Calories: 350, Fat: 5g, Carbohydrates: 70g, Protein: 8g, Fiber: 6g, Sugars: 20g

TIPS:

If you're looking for some added texture and protein, try throwing in a handful of chopped nuts or seeds.

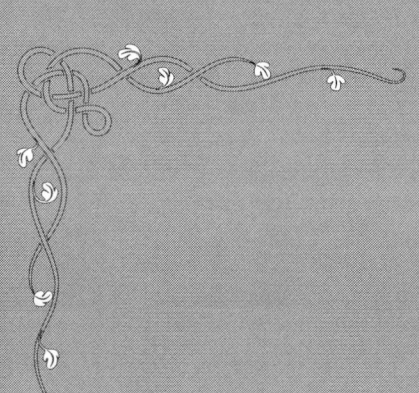
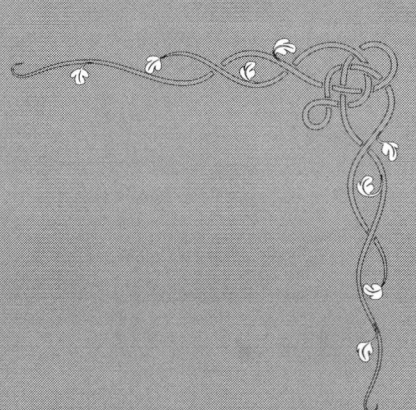

BANANA AND WALNUT MUFFINS

Prep time:
5 minutes

Cooking Time:
20 minutes

Servings:
12 Muffins

INGREDIENTS:

- 2 ripe bananas
- 2 eggs
- 1/2 cup of coconut oil
- 1/4 cup of almond milk
- 1 cup of almond flour
- 1/2 cup of chopped walnuts
- 1 teaspoon of baking soda
- 1 teaspoon of vanilla extract

NUTRITIONS:

Calories: 200, Fat: 15g, Carbohydrates: 12g, Protein: 5g, Fiber: 3g, Sugars: 7g

TIPS:

if dried fruit is more up your alley, swap the walnuts out and replace them with whatever type suits you best.

DIRECTIONS:

1. Heat the oven to 350°F (175°C) and line a muffin tin with paper liners.
2. Grab a bowl, mash up those ripe bananas then crack in two eggs. Throw in some coconut oil, almond milk and vanilla extract blending until you have achieved a smooth mixture.
3. Stir in the almond flour and baking soda fully incorporating all dry ingredients.
4. Now add chopped walnuts; mix it through one last time before filling each liner with your batter.
5. Pop them into the preheated oven for 20 minutes or until golden brown when tested by inserting a toothpick into their centre - if it comes out clean you know they are done!
6. Leave them to cool in the tin for 5 minutes before transferring onto wire racks to complete cooling off completely so that they can be enjoyed at their best!

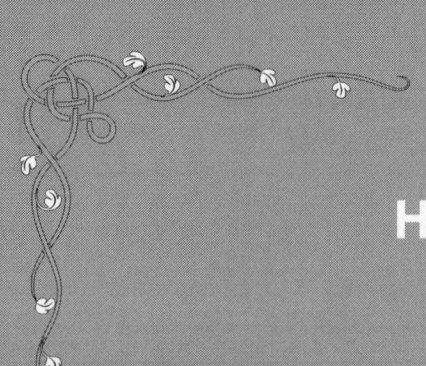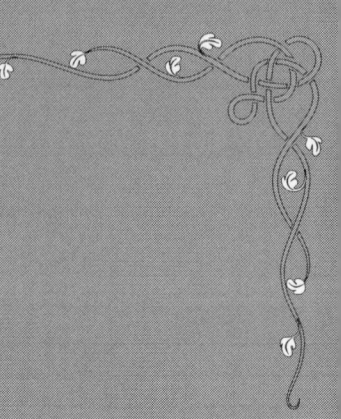

HOMEMADE GLUTEN-FREE GRANOLA

Prep time:
10 minutes

Cooking Time:
30 minutes

Servings:
10

INGREDIENTS:

- 3 cups of gluten-free oats
- 1 cup of chopped walnuts
- 1/2 cup of honey
- 1/4 cup of coconut oil
- 1 teaspoon of cinnamon
- 1/2 cup of raisins

DIRECTIONS:

1. Preheat the oven to 300°F (150°C) and line a baking sheet with parchment paper.
2. In a large bowl, mix the oats, walnuts, and cinnamon.
3. In a saucepan, melt the honey and coconut oil over low heat. Pour the honey and coconut oil mixture over the oats and mix well.
4. Spread the oats on the baking sheet in an even layer.
5. Bake for 30 minutes, stirring every 10 minutes, until the granola is golden.
6. Remove the granola from the oven and let it cool completely. Add the raisins.
7. Store the granola in an airtight container at room temperature.

NUTRITIONS:

Calories: 280, Fat: 14g, Carbohydrates: 36g, Protein: 6g, Fiber: 4g, Sugars: 18g

TIPS:

You can also customize this granola however way you'd like by mixing in different types of fruits, seeds or spices. Just remember to add it after baking so it doesn't burn!

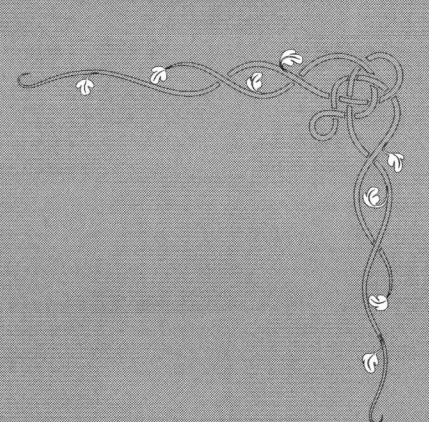

AVOCADO TOAST

Prep time:
10 minutes

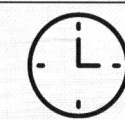
Cooking Time:
00 minutes

Servings:
2

INGREDIENTS:

- 4 slices of gluten-free bread
- 1 ripe avocado
- Juice of 1/2 lemon
- Salt and pepper to taste
- Sesame seeds (optional)

DIRECTIONS:

1. Toast the bread in a toaster until it's golden.
2. In the meantime, mash the avocado in a bowl. Add the lemon juice, salt, and pepper. Mix well.
3. Spread the mashed avocado on the toasted bread slices.
4. Sprinkle with sesame seeds, if desired, and serve immediately

NUTRITIONS:

Calories: 320, Fat: 20g, Carbohydrates: 30g, Protein: 6g, Fiber: 9g, Sugars: 3g

TIPS:

top with either a scrambled egg or slice up a juicy tomato for even more flavor and nutrition!

FRUIT AND GRANOLA YOGURT

 **Prep time:** 5 minutes

 **Cooking Time:** 00 minutes

 **Servings:** 1

INGREDIENTS:
- 1 cup of fat-free Greek yogurt
- 1/2 cup of gluten-free granola
- 1/2 cup of fresh fruit (strawberries, blueberries, bananas, etc.)

DIRECTIONS:
1. In a bowl or glass, layer the yogurt, granola, and fruit.
2. Serve immediately.

NUTRITIONS:
Calories: 350, Fat: 7g, Carbohydrates: 55g, Protein: 20g, Fiber: 5g, Sugars: 25g

TIPS:
for an extra touch of sweetness, try drizzling on some honey or maple syrup.

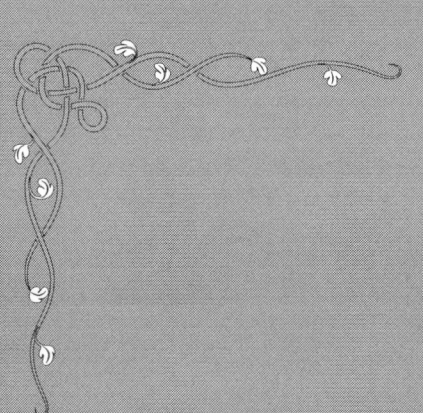
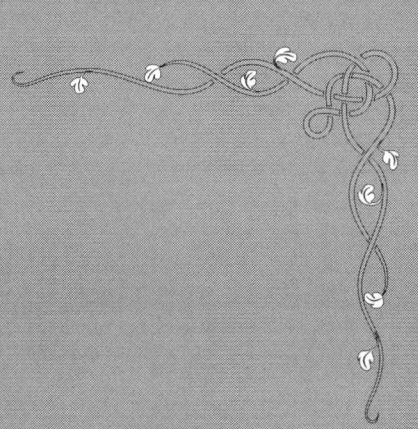

VEGETABLE QUICHE

 **Prep time:** 20 minutes	 **Cooking Time:** 40 minutes	 **Servings:** 6

INGREDIENTS:

- 1 ready-to-use gluten-free pie crust
- 1 cup of fresh spinach
- 1/2 cup of cherry tomatoes, halved
- 1/2 cup of grated cheddar cheese
- 4 eggs
- 1 cup of milk
- Salt and pepper to taste

DIRECTIONS:

1. Preheat the oven to 375°F (190°C).
2. Arrange the pie crust in a quiche dish or pie plate.
3. Distribute the spinach, tomatoes, and cheese on the pie crust.
4. In a bowl, beat the eggs with the milk, salt, and pepper. Pour the egg mixture over the pie crust.
5. Bake for 40 minutes, or until the quiche is golden and cooked.
6. Let it cool for a few minutes before cutting and serving.

NUTRITIONS:

Calories: 250, Fat: 15g, Carbohydrates: 20g, Protein: 10g, Fiber: 2g, Sugars: 3g

TIPS:

you can get creative with your quiche by adding unique veggies and if you want to up the protein content, you could throw in some chicken or ham.

SWEET POTATO PANCAKES

Prep time:
15 minutes

Cooking Time:
20 minutes

Servings:
4

INGREDIENTS:

- 2 medium sweet potatoes, peeled and grated
- 2 eggs
- 1/4 cup of almond flour
- 1/2 teaspoon of cinnamon
- Coconut oil for cooking
- Maple syrup for serving

DIRECTIONS:

1. In a bowl, mix the grated sweet potatoes, eggs, almond flour, and cinnamon.
2. Heat some coconut oil in a non-stick pan over medium heat.
3. Take a spoonful of batter for each pancake and cook for 3-4 minutes per side, or until they are golden.
4. Serve the pancakes hot with a drizzle of maple syrup.

NUTRITIONS:

Calories: 220, Fat: 8g, Carbohydrates: 32g, Protein: 6g, Fiber: 5g, Sugars: 8g

TIPS:

pancakes are also great with something special - why not sprinkle on chopped nuts or seeds for added crunch? Plus, adding a pinch of nutmeg and ginger will take your pancakes from boring to bomb.

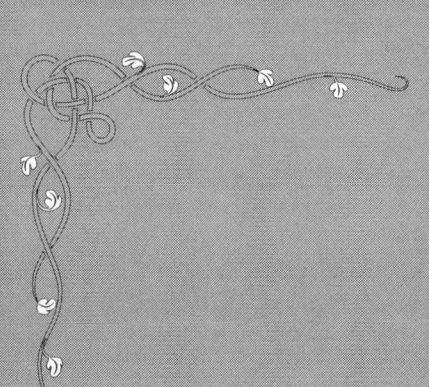
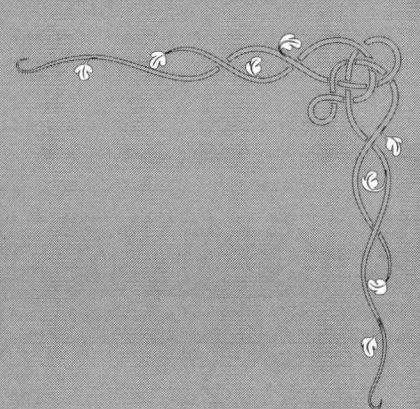

COCONUT AND BERRY SMOOTHIE BOWL

Prep time:
10 minutes

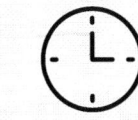
Cooking Time:
00 minutes

Servings:
2

INGREDIENTS:

- 1 frozen banana
- 1 cup of mixed frozen berries (strawberries, blueberries, raspberries, etc.)
- 1 cup of coconut milk
- 2 tablespoons of coconut flakes
- 2 tablespoons of chia seeds
- Fresh fruit for garnish (banana slices, blueberries, raspberries, etc.)

DIRECTIONS:

1. In a blender, blend together the frozen banana, mixed berries, and coconut milk until you get a creamy mixture.
2. Pour the smoothie into two bowls.
3. Garnish with coconut flakes, chia seeds, and fresh fruit.
4. Serve immediately.

NUTRITIONS:

Calories: 250, Fat: 14g, Carbohydrates: 28g, Protein: 4g, Fiber: 8g, Sugars: 14g

TIPS:

you can add gluten-free granola or dried fruit for an extra crunch.

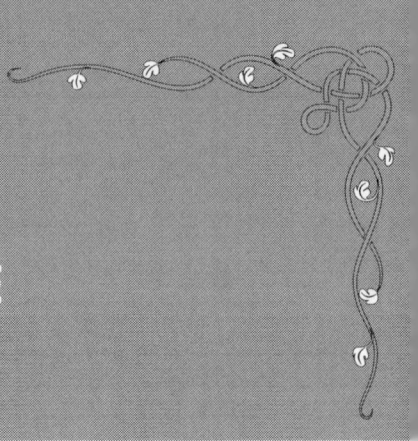

SCRAMBLED EGGS WITH VEGETABLES AND CHEESE

Prep time:
10 minutes

Cooking Time:
10 minutes

Servings:
2

INGREDIENTS:

- 4 eggs
- 2 tablespoons of milk
- 1/4 of a red bell pepper, diced
- 1/4 of a red onion, thinly sliced
- 1/4 cup of fresh spinach
- 1/4 cup of gluten-free grated cheese (cheddar, Swiss, etc.)
- Salt and pepper to taste
- Olive oil for cooking

DIRECTIONS:

1. In a bowl, beat the eggs with the milk, salt, and pepper.
2. Heat a bit of olive oil in a non-stick pan over medium heat. Add the bell pepper and onion and cook for a few minutes, until the vegetables are tender.
3. Add the spinach to the pan and cook until it wilts slightly.
4. Pour the beaten egg into the pan and gently stir with the vegetables.
5. Continue stirring until the eggs are cooked but still soft.
6. Add the grated cheese and stir until it melts.
7. Transfer the scrambled eggs to two plates and serve hot.

NUTRITIONS:

Calories: 280, Fat: 20g, Carbohydrates: 6g, Protein: 18g, Fiber: 2g, Sugars: 3g

TIPS:

you can add other vegetables like diced tomatoes or mushrooms for a flavor-packed punch.

Lunch

BLACK BEAN AND QUINOA SALAD

Prep time:
15 minutes

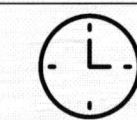
Cooking Time:
15 minutes

Servings:
4

INGREDIENTS:

- 1 cup of quinoa
- 2 cups of water
- 1 can of black beans, drained and rinsed
- 1 red bell pepper, diced
- 1 green onion, chopped • 1 teaspoon of cumin
- Juice of 1 lime
- 3 tablespoons of olive oil
- Salt and pepper to taste

DIRECTIONS:

1. Rinse the quinoa under cold water and drain. Put it in a pot with the water and bring to a boil. Reduce the heat, cover, and let simmer for 15-20 minutes or until the water is absorbed.
2. In a large bowl, combine the cooked quinoa, black beans, red bell pepper, and green onion.
3. In a small bowl, mix the cumin, lime juice, olive oil, salt, and pepper. Pour the dressing over the salad and mix well.

NUTRITIONS:

calories 350, carbohydrates 55g, fat 10g, protein 15g, fiber 10g, sugars 5g.

TIPS:

you can add corn or grilled chicken for an extra flavor and protein boost.

POTATO AND LEEK SOUP

Prep time:
10 minutes

Cooking Time:
30 minutes

Servings:
4

INGREDIENTS:

- • 2 leeks, cleaned and sliced
- • 2 large potatoes, peeled and diced
- • 4 cups of gluten-free vegetable broth
- • 2 tablespoons of olive oil
- • Salt and pepper to taste

DIRECTIONS:

1. In a large pot, heat the olive oil over medium heat. Add the leeks and cook until they become soft, about 5 minutes.
2. Add the potatoes and vegetable broth. Bring to a boil, then reduce the heat and let simmer until the potatoes are tender, about 20 minutes.
3. Use an immersion blender to blend the soup until it reaches a smooth consistency. Season with salt and pepper to taste.

NUTRITIONS:

calories 220, carbohydrates 40g, fat 5g, protein 4g, fiber 5g, sugars 3g

TIPS:

when it comes to leek soup - sautéing those leeks with garlic is key for giving that yummy flavour boost! If you're wanting something creamier then swap out regular milk for lactose-free milk (or almond milk) at the end of cooking time; just remember to adjust seasoning accordingly afterwards.

GRILLED CHICKEN AND AVOCADO SANDWICH

 **Prep time:** 10 minutes | 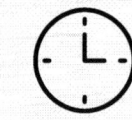 **Cooking Time:** 15 minutes |  **Servings:** 2

INGREDIENTS:

- 2 chicken breasts
- 1 ripe avocado
- 2 gluten-free buns
- 1 tomato
- Lettuce leaves
- 1 tablespoon of olive oil
- Salt and pepper to taste

DIRECTIONS:

1. Heat a grill or non-stick pan over medium-high heat. Season the chicken breasts with olive oil, salt, and pepper, then grill for about 7 minutes per side, or until no longer pink in the center.
2. While the chicken is cooking, slice the avocado and tomato.
3. Once cooked, let the chicken rest for a few minutes, then slice it into thin strips.
4. Assemble the sandwiches with lettuce, tomato, chicken, and avocado.

NUTRITIONS:

Calories 450, Carbohydrates 30g, Fat 20g, Protein 40g, Fiber 10g, Sugars 5g.

TIPS:

Squeeze in some fresh lime juice to add a bit of acidic zing to the avocado. For an extra cheesy flavor, top off your hot chicken with a slice of lactose-free cheese and let it melt right in!

LENTIL AND VEGETABLE SOUP

Prep time: 10 minutes

Cooking Time: 40 minutes

Servings: 4

INGREDIENTS:

- 1 cup of lentils
- 1 carrot, diced
- 2 celery stalks, diced
- 1 onion, chopped
- 4 cups of gluten-free vegetable broth
- 1 teaspoon of cumin
- 2 tablespoons of olive oil
- Salt and pepper to taste

DIRECTIONS:

1. In a large pot, heat the olive oil over medium heat. Add the carrot, celery, and onion, and cook until the vegetables are tender, about 5 minutes.
2. Add the lentils, vegetable broth, and cumin. Bring to a boil, then reduce the heat and let simmer until the lentils are tender, about 30 minutes.
3. Season with salt and pepper to taste.

NUTRITIONS:

Calories 210, Carbohydrates 35g, Fat 3g, Protein 14g, Fiber 15g, Sugars 4g.

TIPS:

if you're feeling adventurous, swap out the cumin for smoked paprika for that smoky kick. Once you've enjoyed your soup, garnish it with some chopped parsley or cilantro - this will introduce a burst of vibrant flavor.

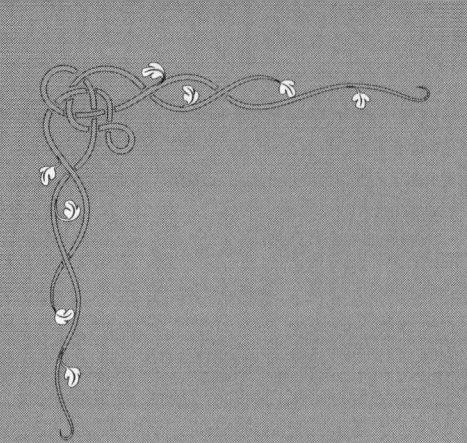

MUSHROOM RISOTTO

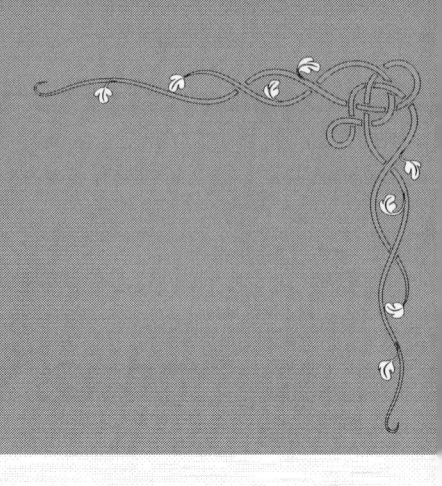

Prep time: 10 minutes

Cooking Time: 30 minutes

Servings: 4

INGREDIENTS:

- 1 cup of Arborio rice
- 4 cups of gluten-free vegetable broth
- 2 cups of mixed mushrooms, sliced
- 1 small onion, chopped
- 2 tablespoons of olive oil
- 1/2 cup of dry white wine
- Salt and pepper to taste

DIRECTIONS:

1. In a large pot, heat the olive oil over medium heat. Add the onion and cook until it becomes transparent, about 5 minutes.
2. Add the mushrooms and cook until they become golden, about 5 minutes.
3. Add the rice and cook for 2 minutes, then add the wine and cook until it's almost completely evaporated.
4. Add the broth, one cup at a time, cooking and stirring until each cup of broth is absorbed before adding the next.
5. Continue to cook until the rice is tender and creamy. Season with salt and pepper to taste.

NUTRITIONS:

Calories 370, Carbohydrates 60g, Fat 10g, Protein 8g, Fiber 3g, Sugars 2g.

TIPS:

feeling creative? Jazz up your risotto by throwing in any type of mushrooms you fancy. To add even more deliciousness on top (literally!), sprinkle over some grated lactose-free cheese or chopped parsley when serving.

GRILLED FISH TACOS

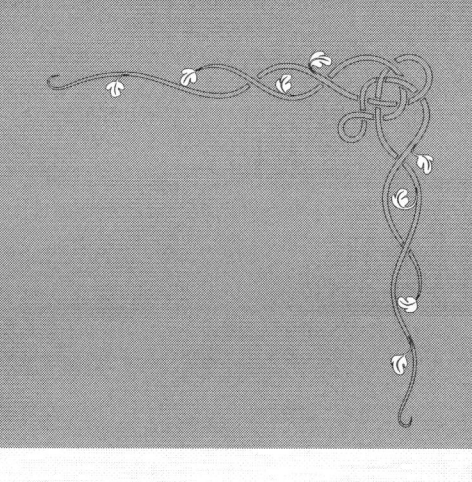

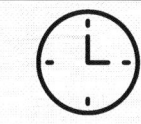

Prep time: 15 minutes

Cooking Time: 10 minutes

Servings: 4

INGREDIENTS:

- 1.1 lb of white fish fillet
- 8 gluten-free corn tortillas
- 1 avocado, sliced
- 1 lime, cut into wedges
- 1 tablespoon of olive oil
- Salt and pepper to taste

DIRECTIONS:

1. Heat a grill or non-stick pan over medium-high heat. Season the fish with olive oil, salt, and pepper, then grill for about 4 minutes per side, or until the fish is cooked and flakes easily with a fork.
2. Warm the tortillas on the grill for about 30 seconds per side, then fill each with the fish, avocado, and a squeeze of lime juice.

NUTRITIONS:

Calories 400, Carbohydrates 35g, Fat 15g, Protein 30g, Fiber 7g, Sugars 2g

TIPS:

tacos are all about personalization so go wild - drizzle them with hot sauce or dollop on some lactose-free yogurt sauce if that's what rocks your boat! Throw together whatever salad ingredients take your fancy and dice up those juicy tomatoes for an extra pop of flavour!

TERIYAKI CHICKEN WITH RICE

Prep time: 10 minutes

Cooking Time: 20 minutes

Servings: 4

INGREDIENTS:

- 4 chicken breasts
- 1 cup of gluten-free teriyaki sauce
- 2 cups of basmati rice
- 1 broccoli, cut into florets
- 1 tablespoon of olive oil
- Sesame seeds for garnish

DIRECTIONS:

1. In a large pan, heat the olive oil over medium-high heat. Add the chicken breasts and cook for about 7 minutes per side, or until no longer pink in the center.
2. While the chicken is cooking, cook the rice according to the package Directions.
3. In a separate pot, steam the broccoli until it becomes bright and tender.
4. Once cooked, pour the teriyaki sauce over the chicken and let it simmer for a couple of minutes.
5. Serve the chicken with the rice and broccoli, and garnish with sesame seeds.

NUTRITIONS:

Calories 500, Carbohydrates 60g, Fats 10g, Proteins 40g, Fiber 5g, Sugars 10g.

TIPS:

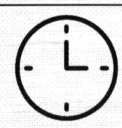

you can jazz up this dish with some additional veggies like carrots or bell peppers for a nutritious boost. For an extra hint of freshness, you could garnish it with chopped green onions.

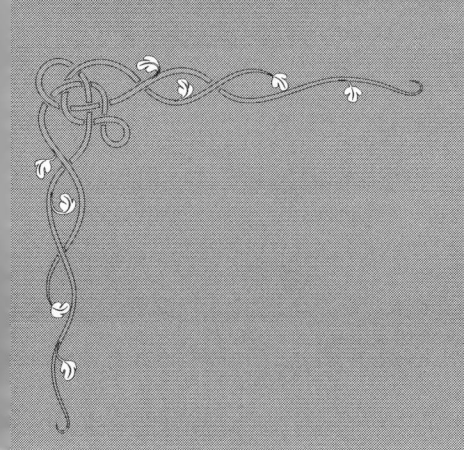

PRIMAVERA PASTA

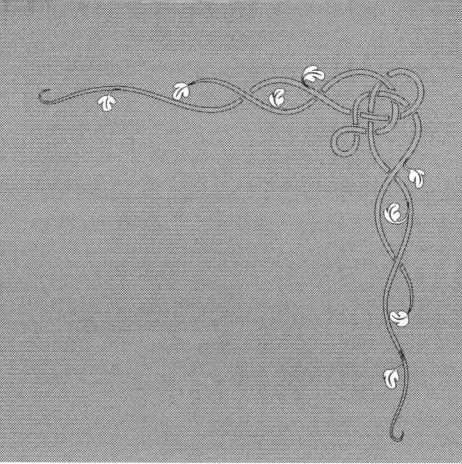

Prep time: 10 minutes

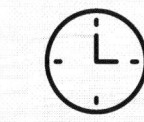

Cooking Time: 15 minutes

Servings: 4

INGREDIENTS:
- 14 ounces of gluten-free pasta
- 1 zucchini, sliced
- 1 carrot, sliced
- 1 red bell pepper, sliced
- 2 tablespoons of olive oil
- 2 cloves of garlic, minced
- Salt and pepper to taste

DIRECTIONS:
1. Cook the pasta according to the package Directions.
2. While the pasta is cooking, heat the olive oil in a large pan over medium heat. Add the garlic and cook until it becomes fragrant, about 1 minute.
3. Add the zucchini, carrot, and bell pepper, and cook until the vegetables become tender, about 5 minutes.
4. Drain the pasta, then add it to the pan with the vegetables. Stir well to combine, then season with salt and pepper to taste.

NUTRITIONS:
Calories 400, Carbohydrates 70g, Fats 10g, Proteins 10g, Fiber 5g, Sugars 6g.

TIPS:
if you really want to take things up a notch, add in some diced chili pepper for that spicy kick! Parsley and lactose-free cheese are also great options if you're looking to give the pasta primavera an added flavor twist. This meal is so versatile - feel free to mix and match whatever seasonal produce your heart desires!

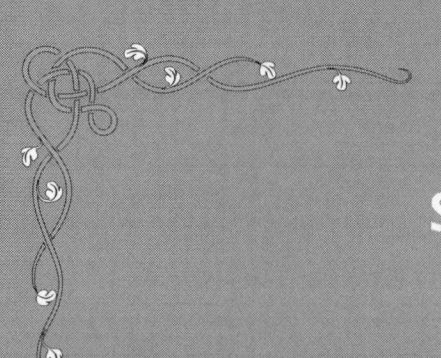

SPINACH AND TOMATO FRITTATA

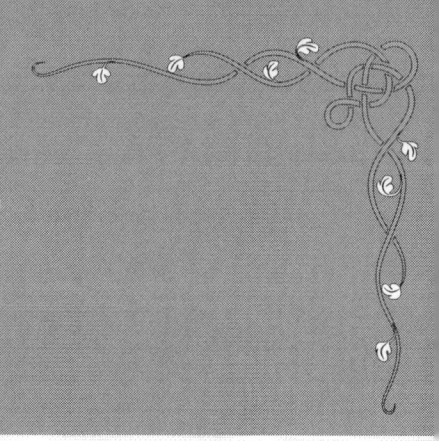

Prep time: 10 minutes

Cooking Time: 15 minutes

Servings: 4

INGREDIENTS:

- 6 large eggs
- 2 cups of fresh spinach
- 1 large tomato, sliced
- 1 small onion, chopped
- 2 tablespoons of olive oil
- Salt and pepper to taste

DIRECTIONS:

1. In a non-stick pan, heat the olive oil over medium heat. Add the onion and cook until it becomes transparent, about 5 minutes.
2. Add the spinach and cook until it wilts, about 2 minutes.
3. In a bowl, beat the eggs and season with salt and pepper. Pour the eggs into the pan with the spinach and onion, then arrange the tomato slices on top.
4. Reduce the heat to medium-low, cover the pan and let it cook until the eggs are fully cooked, about 10 minutes.

NUTRITIONS:

Calories 200, Carbohydrates 5g, Fats 15g, Proteins 12g, Fiber 1g, Sugars 3g.

TIPS:

when it comes to frittata, you're only limited by your imagination; feel free to toss in bell peppers or zucchini if you want extra nutrients and finish off with a sprinkle of parsley for freshness.

GREEK CHICKEN SALAD

Prep time: 15 minutes

Cooking Time: 00 minutes

Servings: 4

INGREDIENTS:

- 2 grilled chicken breasts, sliced
- 1 romaine lettuce, cut into strips
- 1 cucumber, sliced
- 2 tomatoes, sliced
- 1/2 red onion, finely sliced
- 1/2 cup of Kalamata olives
- 1/2 cup of lactose-free feta cheese, crumbled
- 3 tablespoons of olive oil
- 1 tablespoon of red wine vinegar
- Salt and pepper to taste

DIRECTIONS:

1. In a large bowl, combine the lettuce, cucumber, tomatoes, onion, olives, feta cheese, and chicken.
2. In a small bowl, mix the olive oil, red wine vinegar, salt, and pepper. Pour the dressing over the salad and mix well.

NUTRITIONS:

Calories 350, Carbohydrates 10g, Fats 20g, Proteins 30g, Fiber 3g, Sugars 5g.

TIPS:

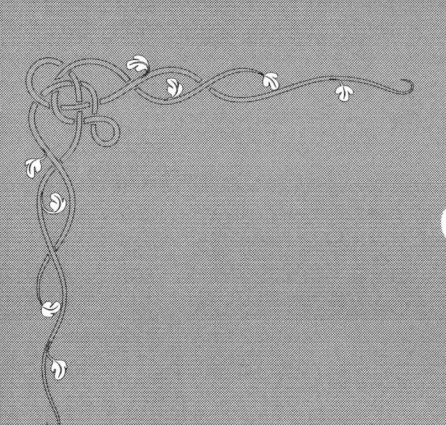

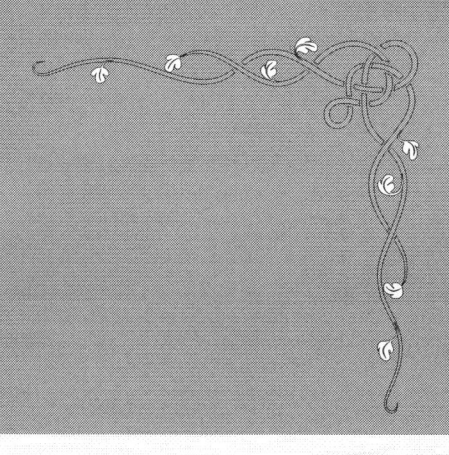

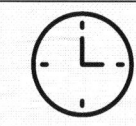

when making Greek chicken salad, don't forget about adding herbs such as oregano or mint for authentic Mediterranean flair. If poultry isn't your thing, switch out the chicken cubes with grilled tofu instead – perfect for vegetarian diets! A sprinkle of parsley on top will help bring out its refreshing qualities too; ideal when summer's around the corner!

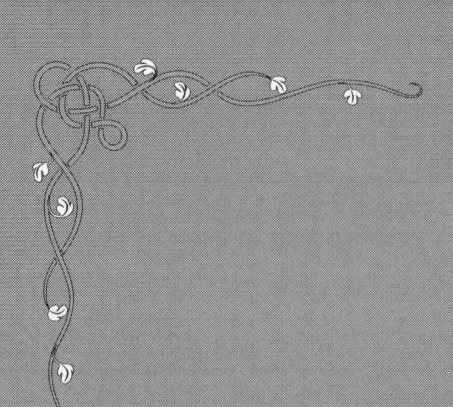

TURKEY AND QUINOA MEATBALLS

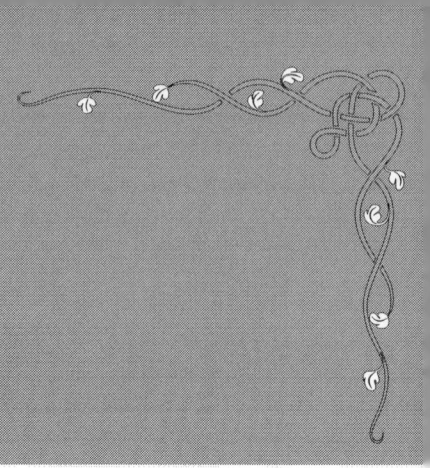

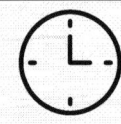

Prep time: 15 minutes

Cooking Time: 20 minutes

Servings: 4

INGREDIENTS:
- 1 lb of turkey breast
- 1 cup of cooked quinoa
- 1 egg
- 1 small onion, chopped
- 2 cloves of garlic, chopped
- 1 tablespoon of olive oil
- Salt and pepper to taste

DIRECTIONS:
1. Preheat the oven to 390°F and line a baking sheet with parchment paper.
2. Take the turkey breast and cut it into cubes, then use a chopper or blender to grind it.
3. In a large bowl, combine the ground turkey, quinoa, egg, onion, andgarlic. Season with salt and pepper, then mix until the ingredients are well combined.
4. Form meatballs with the mixture and place them on the prepared baking sheet.
5. Bake in the preheated oven for 20 minutes, or until the meatballs are fully cooked.

NUTRITIONS:
Calories 350, Carbohydrates 30g, Fats 10g, Proteins 30g, Fiber 3g, Sugars 2g.

TIPS:
you can serve them up with either lactose-free yogurt sauce or gluten-free tomato sauce – perfect for meal prep!

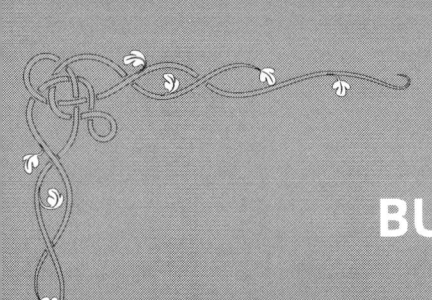

BUCKWHEAT AND ROASTED VEGETABLE SALAD

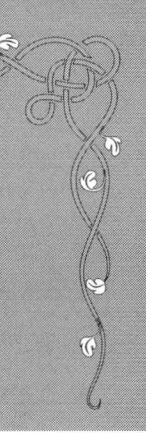

Prep time: 15 minutes

Cooking Time: 30 minutes

Servings: 4

INGREDIENTS:

- 1 cup of buckwheat
- 2 cups of water
- 1 zucchini, sliced
- 1 red pepper, sliced
- 1 red onion, sliced
- 3 tablespoons of olive oil
- Salt and pepper to taste

NUTRITIONS:

Calories 350, Carbohydrates 60g, Fats 10g, Proteins 10g, Fiber 8g, Sugars 5g.

TIPS:

You can add other seasonal vegetables to your salad, like carrots or asparagus. For a protein boost, consider adding chickpeas or lentils. If you prefer, you can also dress the salad with a bit of balsamic vinegar or lemon juice for a touch of acidity.

DIRECTIONS:

1. Preheat your oven to 200°C and prepare a baking tray by lining it with parchment paper.
2. Place the zucchini, pepper, and onion evenly on the sheet before drizzling over 2 tablespoons of olive oil.
3. Sprinkle salt and pepper for seasoning then roast in the preheated oven for 20-30 minutes until tender yet caramelized.
4. While those are cooking away, get your buckwheat ready - put it into a pot along with enough water to cover it all up. Let this boil then reduce heat and let simmer uncovered for 15-20 minutes or until absorbed all that liquid goodness.
5. Once cooked through, combine everything together: mix in roasted vegetables plus add some more olive oil if you like as well as additional seasonings (salt and pepper) according to taste preference.

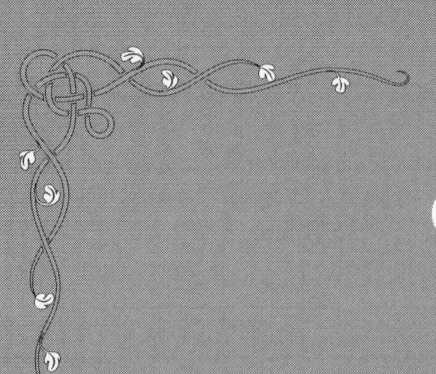

QUINOA WITH GRILLED VEGETABLES

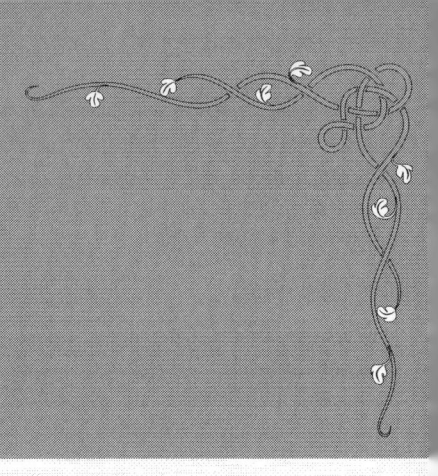

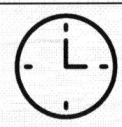

Prep time: 15 minutes

Cooking Time: 20 minutes

Servings: 4

INGREDIENTS:

- 1 cup of quinoa
- 2 cups of water
- 1 zucchini, sliced
- 1 red pepper, sliced
- 1 red onion, sliced
- 3 tablespoons of olive oil
- Salt and pepper to taste

DIRECTIONS:

1. Heat up a pot and bring the quinoa and water to a vigorous boil. Reduce the flame, cover it, then simmer for 15-20 minutes until all of the liquid has been absorbed.
2. While that's cooking away, fire up your grill or non-stick pan over medium-high heat. Char each side of zucchini slices, peppers and onions till they are softened with some nice color around them - about five minutes per side should do it.
3. Combine all of those grilled veggies with your cooked quinoa in one bowl before tossing everything together with olive oil, salt & pepper to taste. Enjoy.

NUTRITIONS:

Calories 300, Carbohydrates 40g, Fats 10g, Proteins 8g, Fiber 5g, Sugars 5g.

TIPS:

You can add other grilled vegetables like asparagus or eggplant. For a protein-packed punch, add some chickpeas or lentils - perfect for those looking to up their plant-based game.

CURRY CHICKEN WITH BASMATI RICE

Prep time: 10 minutes

Cooking Time: 30 minutes

Servings: 4

INGREDIENTS:

- 4 chicken breasts, cubed
- 2 tablespoons of curry powder
- 1 onion, chopped
- 2 cloves of garlic, chopped
- 1 cup of coconut milk
- 2 cups of basmati rice
- 3 tablespoons of olive oil
- Salt and pepper to taste

DIRECTIONS:

1. In a large pot, heat 2 tablespoons of olive oil over medium heat. Add the onion and garlicand cook until they become transparent, about 5 minutes.
2. Add the chicken and curry powder, then cook until the chicken is no longer pink, about 7 minutes.
3. Add the coconut milk, then reduce the heat to medium-low and simmer for 15 minutes.
4. While the chicken is cooking, cook the basmati rice according to the Directions on the package.
5. Serve the curry chicken over the cooked basmati rice.

NUTRITIONS:

Calories 500, Carbohydrates 50g, Fats 20g, Proteins 30g, Fiber 3g, Sugars 3g.

TIPS:

for an extra special twist, try adding a squeeze of lime juice and sprinkling some freshly chopped cilantro to your curry chicken. This will give the dish a vibrant flavor that perfectly contrasts with its savory richness.

SPINACH AND FETA FRITTATA

Prep time: 10 minutes

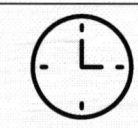

Cooking Time: 20 minutes

Servings: 4

INGREDIENTS:

- 6 large eggs
- 1 cup of fresh spinach
- 1/2 cup of crumbled feta cheese
- 1 small onion, chopped
- 2 tablespoons of olive oil
- Salt and pepper to taste

NUTRITIONS:

Calories 250, Carbohydrates 5g, Fats 18g, Proteins 16g, Fiber 1g, Sugars 2g.

TIPS:

If you're feeling adventurous, why not throw in a bit of chopped chilli and smoked feta cheese? Don't forget tomatoes and bell peppers too - they'll bring an extra depth of flavor.

DIRECTIONS:

1. Heat up the oven and set it to 350°F.
2. In a non-stick, oven-safe skillet, warm some olive oil over medium heat. Toss in the chopped onion and let it cook until translucent - about five minutes.
3. Put the spinach into the pan and stir occasionally till wilted - approximately two minutes.
4. Crack open a few eggs in a bowl then add feta cheese, pepper, and salt; pour this mixture onto onions & spinach in skillet once done stirring everything together evenly.
5. Place frittata inside preheated oven for 15-20 mins or until eggs become fully cooked through.

Dinner

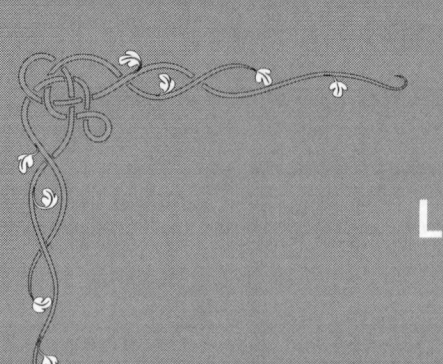

LEMON AND ROSEMARY CHICKEN

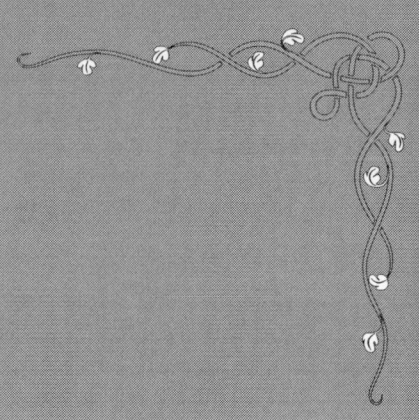

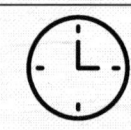

Prep time: 15 minutes

Cooking Time: 45 minutes

Servings: 4

INGREDIENTS:

- 4 skinless chicken breasts
- 2 lemons
- 4 sprigs of fresh rosemary
- 2 tablespoons of olive oil
- Salt and black pepper to taste
- 2 cloves of garlic

DIRECTIONS:

1. Preheat the oven to 375°F (190°C).
2. Rub the chicken breasts with the juice of one lemon, salt, pepper, and a tablespoon of olive oil.
3. Arrange the chicken breasts in a baking dish and add the rosemary sprigs and garlic cloves.
4. Slice the remaining lemon into thin slices and place them over the chicken.
5. Bake and cook for 45 minutes or until the chicken is no longer pink in the center.
6. Serve hot.

NUTRITIONS:

Calories 265, Carbohydrates 3g, Fat 14g, Protein 30g, Fiber 1g, Sugars 1g.

TIPS:

why not pair it with grilled vegetables or throw together a fresh green salad?

BAKED SALMON WITH HONEY MUSTARD SAUCE

Prep time: 10 minutes

Cooking Time: 20 minutes

Servings: 4

INGREDIENTS:

- 4 salmon fillets (about 6 ounces each)
- 2 tablespoons of Dijon mustard
- 2 tablespoons of honey
- 1 tablespoon of olive oil
- Salt and black pepper to taste
- 1 lemon, sliced

DIRECTIONS:

1. Preheat the oven to 400°F (200°C).
2. In a small bowl, mix the Dijon mustard, honey, olive oil, salt, and pepper.
3. Arrange the salmon fillets on a baking sheet lined with parchment paper.
4. Spread the mustard and honey mixture on the salmon fillets.
5. Arrange the lemon slices over and around the salmon.
6. Bake for 15-20 minutes, or until the salmon flakes easily with a fork.
7. Serve hot.

NUTRITIONS:

Calories 345, Carbohydrates 9g, Fat 19g, Protein 34g, Fiber 0g, Sugars 7g.

TIPS:

quinoa or steamed veggies make perfect sides.

GRILLED EGGPLANT ROLLS

Prep time: 15 minutes

Cooking Time: 15 minutes

Servings: 4

INGREDIENTS:

- 2 large eggplants
- 2 tablespoons of olive oil
- Salt and black pepper to taste
- 1 cup of ricotta
- 1/2 cup of fresh basil, chopped
- 1/2 cup of sun-dried tomatoes, chopped

DIRECTIONS:

1. Slice the eggplants into long, thin slices. Brush both sides with olive oil and season with salt and pepper.
2. Grill the eggplant slices on a hot grill for 2-3 minutes per side, until they are soft and have nice grill marks.
3. While the eggplants are cooling, mix the ricotta, basil, and sun-dried tomatoes in a bowl.
4. Spread some of the ricotta mixture on each slice of eggplant, then roll up the slices.
5. Serve cold or at room temperature.

NUTRITIONS:

Calories 210, Carbohydrates 15g, Fat 14g, Protein 7g, Fiber 7g, Sugars 8g.

TIPS:

This eggplant roll-up makes a great appetizer or side dish, and can easily be prepped ahead of time and stored in the fridge.

PORK STEAK WITH APPLE SAUCE

Prep time: 10 minutes

Cooking Time: 20 minutes

Servings: 4

INGREDIENTS:

- 4 pork steaks
- Salt and black pepper to taste
- 2 tablespoons of olive oil
- 2 apples, thinly sliced
- 1/2 cup of apple cider
- 1 tablespoon of Dijon mustard
- 1 tablespoon of honey

DIRECTIONS:

1. Season the pork steaks with salt and pepper.
2. Heat the olive oil in a large pan over medium-high heat. Add the pork steaks and cook for 5-7 minutes per side, until they are no longer pink in the center. Remove the steaks from the pan and keep them warm.
3. In the same pan, add the apples and cook until they start to soften. Add the apple cider, Dijon mustard, and honey, and cook until the sauce has reduced by half.
4. Pour the apple sauce over the pork steaks and serve hot.

NUTRITIONS:

Calories 320, Carbohydrates 15g, Fat 14g, Protein 28g, Fiber 2g, Sugars 12g.

TIPS:

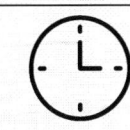

When it comes to pairing this pork steak with apple sauce, roasted sweet potatoes or steamed vegetables are always a winning combo. For an extra flavour boost, try sprinkling a pinch of cinnamon on top!

LENTIL AND SAUSAGE STEW

Prep time: 10 minutes

Cooking Time: 40 minutes

Servings: 4

INGREDIENTS:

- 1 lb of gluten-free pork sausage, cut into rounds
- 1 onion, chopped
- 2 carrots, sliced into rounds
- 2 cloves of garlic, chopped
- 1 cup of green lentils
- 4 cups of gluten-free chicken broth
- Salt and black pepper to taste
- 2 tablespoons of olive oil
- 1 tablespoon of fresh thyme, chopped

DIRECTIONS:

1. Heat the olive oil in a large pot over medium-high heat. Add the sausage and cook until it is no longer pink.
2. Add the onion, carrots, and garlic, and cook until the onion is transparent.
3. Add the lentils, chicken broth, salt, pepper, and thyme, then bring to a boil. Reduce the heat, cover, and simmer for 30 minutes, or until the lentils are tender.
4. Serve hot, with a sprinkle of fresh thyme.

NUTRITIONS:

Calories 450, Carbohydrates 40g, Fat 20g, Protein 25g, Fiber 15g, Sugars 4g.

TIPS:

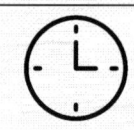

This stew is all the meal you need right there; but why not add some extra oomph by serving it up with some delicious gluten free bread? Just don't forget to check that your sausage is gluten-free!

GRILLED SHRIMP WITH GARLIC SAUCE

Prep time: 15 minutes

Cooking Time: 10 minutes

Servings: 4

INGREDIENTS:

- 1 lb of large shrimp, peeled and deveined
- 2 tablespoons of olive oil
- Salt and black pepper to taste
- 4 cloves of garlic, chopped
- 1 lemon, sliced
- Chopped fresh parsley, for garnish

DIRECTIONS:

1. Preheat the grill to medium-high heat.
2. In a large bowl, mix the shrimp with the olive oil, garlic, salt, and pepper.
3. Thread the shrimp onto skewers, then grill for 2-3 minutes per side, or until the shrimp turn pink and opaque.
4. Serve the grilled shrimp with the lemon slices and a sprinkle of fresh parsley.

NUTRITIONS:

Calories 180, Carbohydrates 2g, Fat 8g, Protein 24g, Fiber 0g, Sugars 1g.

TIPS:

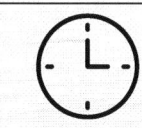

These grilled shrimps are a zesty and wholesome dish, ideal for an al fresco dinner. Serve them alongside some brown rice or a colorful salad to make it extra delectable!

TERIYAKI CHICKEN

Prep time: 15 minutes

Cooking Time: 20 minutes

Servings: 4

INGREDIENTS:

- 4 skinless chicken breasts
- 1/2 cup of gluten-free teriyaki sauce
- 1 tablespoon of olive oil
- 2 cloves of garlic, chopped
- 1 tablespoon of fresh ginger, grated
- Sesame seeds and chopped green onion, for garnish

DIRECTIONS:

1. In a medium bowl, mix the teriyaki sauce, garlic, and ginger.
2. Add the chicken breasts to the marinade and let rest for at least 10 minutes.
3. Heat the olive oil in a large pan over medium-high heat. Add the chicken breasts and cook for 6-7 minutes per side, or until the chicken is no longer pink in the center.
4. Serve the teriyaki chicken with a sprinkle of sesame seeds and green onion.

NUTRITIONS:

Calories 280, Carbohydrates 10g, Fat 8g, Protein 38g, Fiber 0g, Sugars 8g.

TIPS:

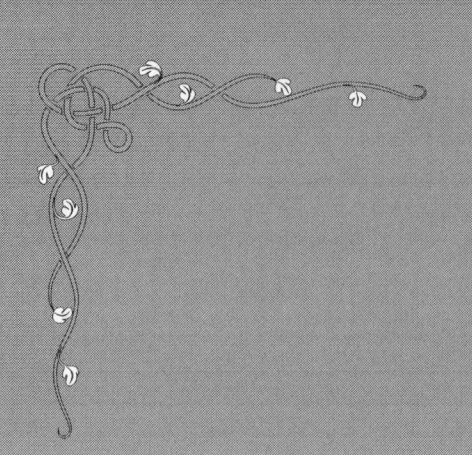

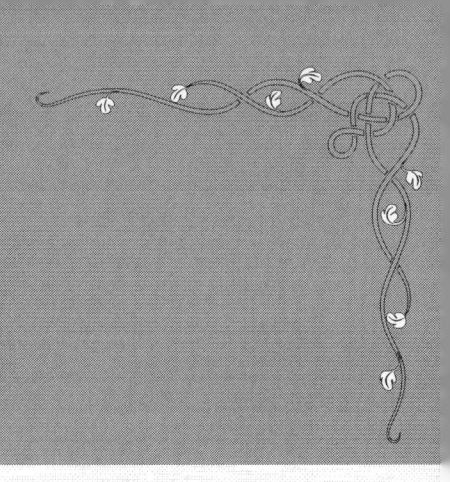

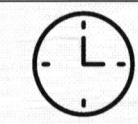

Teriyaki chicken pairs wonderfully with basmati rice or steamed veggies - just be sure the teriyaki sauce is gluten-free.

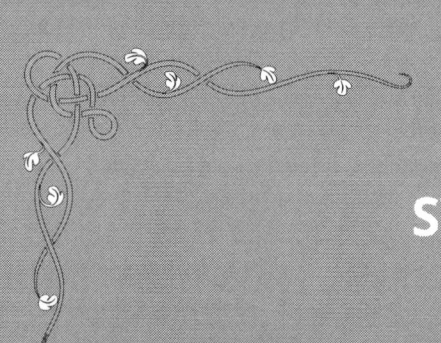

SWEET POTATO AND RED PEPPER SOUP

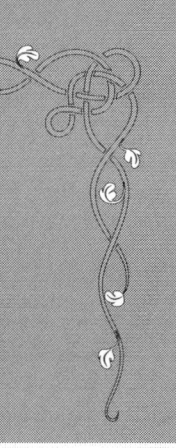

Prep time: 15 minutes	Cooking Time: 30 minutes	Servings: 4

INGREDIENTS:

- 2 large sweet potatoes, peeled and cubed
- 2 red bell peppers, cubed
- 1 onion, chopped
- 2 cloves of garlic, chopped
- 4 cups of gluten-free vegetable broth
- 2 tablespoons of olive oil
- Salt and black pepper to taste
- 1 tablespoon of cumin
- 1 tablespoon of sweet paprika

DIRECTIONS:

1. Heat the olive oil in a large pot over medium heat. Add the onion and garlic, and cook until the onion is transparent.
2. Add the sweet potatoes, red bell peppers, vegetable broth, salt, pepper, cumin, and paprika. Bring to a boil, then reduce the heat, cover, and simmer for 20 minutes, or until the sweet potatoes are tender.
3. Use an immersion blender to blend the soup until it is smooth.
4. Serve hot, with a sprinkle of sweet paprika.

NUTRITIONS:

Calories 220, Carbohydrates 40g, Fat 6g, Protein 4g, Fiber 6g, Sugars 10g.

TIPS:

Soup can be enjoyed as its own meal, but why not go the extra mile and add in some delicious gluten-free bread? Sprinkle in chili powder for that kick of heat if you're feeling adventurous!

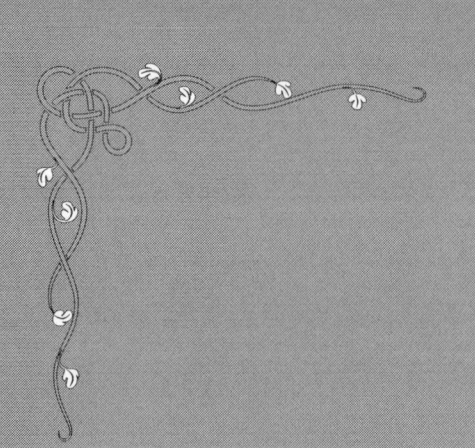

BEEF FAJITAS

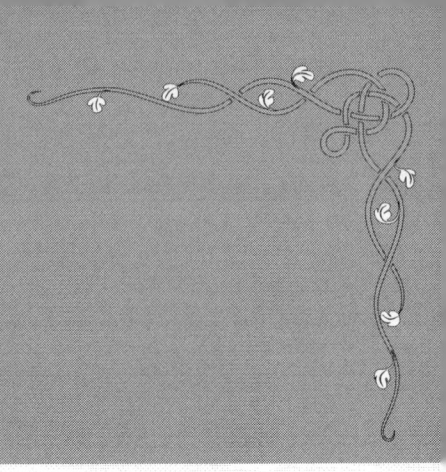

Prep time: 15 minutes	Cooking Time: 15 minutes	Servings: 4

INGREDIENTS:

- 1 lb of beef steak, cut into strips
- 1 tablespoon of olive oil
- 1 onion, sliced
- 2 bell peppers, sliced
- 1 packet of gluten-free fajita spice mix
- 8 gluten-free corn tortillas
- Guacamole, salsa, and fresh cilantro, to serve

DIRECTIONS:

1. Heat the olive oil in a large pan over medium-high heat. Add the steak and cook until it is no longer pink.
2. Add the onion and bell peppers to the pan and cook until they are tender.
3. Add the fajita spice mix and stir well to combine.
4. Warm the tortillas in a dry pan or in the microwave, then fill with the beef and vegetable mixture.
5. Serve the fajitas with guacamole, salsa, and a sprinkle of fresh cilantro.

NUTRITIONS:

Calories 400, Carbohydrates 35g, Fat 15g, Protein 30g, Fiber 5g, Sugars 3g.

TIPS:

Beef fajitas are always fun to whip up at home and customize your way with toppings like sour cream, shredded cheese, black beans - which should all double check their gluten-free status before being added on top.

CHICKPEA AND SPINACH CURRY

Prep time: 10 minutes

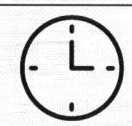

Cooking Time: 20 minutes

Servings: 4

INGREDIENTS:
- 2 cans of chickpeas, drained and rinsed
- 1 onion, chopped
- 2 cloves of garlic, chopped
- 1 tablespoon of olive oil
- 1 tablespoon of curry powder
- 1 teaspoon of turmeric
- 1 teaspoon of cumin
- 1/2 teaspoon of chili powder (optional)
- 1 can of coconut milk
- 4 cups of fresh spinach
- Salt to taste
- Fresh cilantro and cooked basmati rice, toserve

DIRECTIONS:
1. Heat the olive oil in a large pot over medium heat. Add the onion and garlic, and cook until the onion is transparent.
2. Add the curry powder, turmeric, cumin, and chili powder (if using), and cook for another minute.
3. Add the chickpeas and coconut milk to the pot, bring to a boil, then reduce the heat and simmer for 10 minutes.
4. Add the spinach and cook until it has wilted. Adjust the salt.
5. Serve the chickpea and spinach curry on a bed of basmati rice, with a sprinkle of fresh cilantro.

NUTRITIONS:
Calories 350, Carbohydrates 45g, Fat 12g, Protein 12g, Fiber 10g, Sugars 6g.

TIPS:
This chickpea & spinach curry has got everything you need in one bowl; serve it oversteaming hotgluten-free naan for a heartier feast.

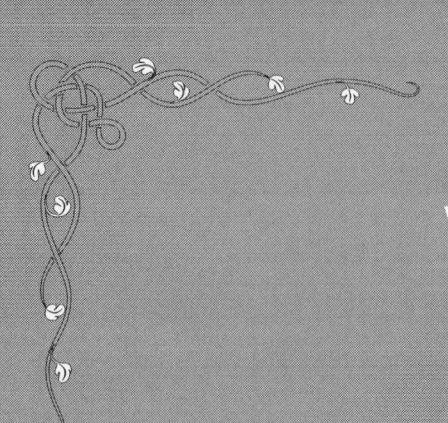

VEGAN BUDDHA BOWL

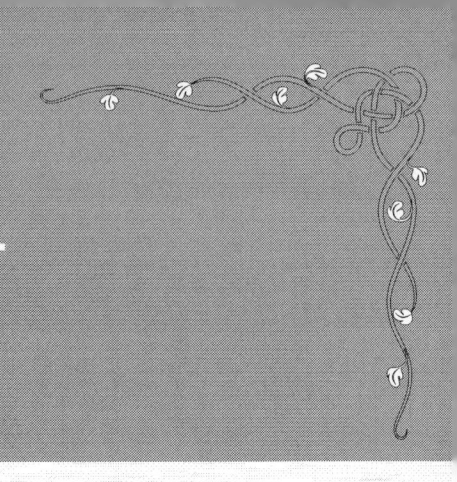

Prep time: 15 minutes

Cooking Time: 30 minutes

Servings: 4

INGREDIENTS:

- 1 cup of quinoa
- 2 cups of gluten-free vegetable broth
- 2 sweet potatoes, cut into cubes
- 1 tablespoon of olive oil
- Salt and black pepper to taste
- 1 can of chickpeas, drained and rinsed
- 2 cups of kale, cut into strips
- 1 avocado, sliced
- Tahini sauce, for serving

NUTRITIONS:

Calories 450, Carbohydrates 65g, Fats 15g, Proteins 15g, Fiber 15g, Sugars 8g.

TIPS:

Try throwing in some toasted pumpkin seeds or roasting some colorful vegetables for extra flavor and nutrition.

DIRECTIONS:

1. Bring the vegetable broth to a boil in a medium pot, then add the quinoa, reduce the heat, cover and cook for 15 minutes, or until the quinoa has absorbed all the broth.
2. In the meantime, preheat the oven to 400°F (200°C) and line a baking sheet with parchment paper.
3. Arrange the sweet potatoes on the baking sheet, season with olive oil, salt and pepper, and bake for 20-25 minutes, or until the sweet potatoes are tender and caramelized.
4. Assemble the Buddha bowls with the quinoa, sweet potatoes, chickpeas, kale, and avocado. Serve with a drizzle of tahini sauce.

HUNTER'S CHICKEN

Prep time: 15 minutes

Cooking Time: 45 minutes

Servings: 4

INGREDIENTS:

- 4 chicken thighs
- Salt and black pepper to taste
- 2 tablespoons of olive oil
- 1 onion, chopped
- 2 cloves of garlic, chopped
- 1 red pepper, cut into strips
- 1 can of peeled tomatoes
- 1/2 cup of red wine
- 1 tablespoon of dried oregano
- Fresh parsley, chopped, for garnish

NUTRITIONS:

Calories 350, Carbohydrates 10g, Fats 20g, Proteins 30g, Fiber 2g, Sugars 5g.

TIPS:

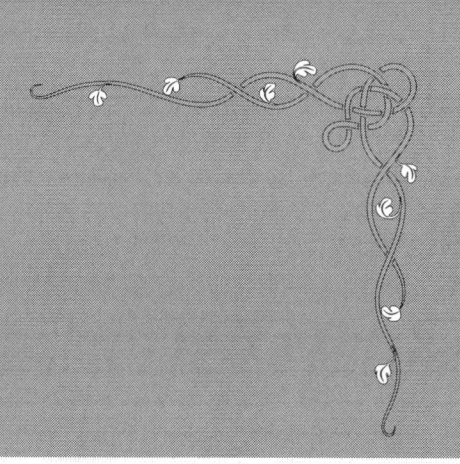

Serve it alongside brown rice or a green salad to create an even more filling meal.

DIRECTIONS:

1. Season the chicken with a generous pinch of salt and pepper, then heat up some olive oil in a large pan over medium-high heat.
2. Throw chicken thighs into the hot pan and fry until they're golden brown on both sides - you'll know it's time to remove them when your kitchen is filled with an amazing aroma.
3. Add in minced onions, garlic cloves, and red peppers; let 'em sizzle until the onion becomes translucent.
4. Pour in some diced peeled tomatoes along with a splash of red wine and oregano for flavor.
5. Now reduce that heat down low so we can cover our skillet before letting everything simmer together for 30 minutes (or until cooked through).
6. Serve the hunter's chicken with a sprinkle of fresh parsley.

GRILLED SALMON WITH LEMON AND PARSLEY SAUCE

Prep time: 10 minutes	Cooking Time: 12 minutes	Servings: 4

INGREDIENTS:

- 4 skinless salmon fillets
- Juice of 2 lemons
- 2 tablespoons of olive oil
- 2 cloves of garlic, chopped
- Fresh parsley, chopped, for garnish
- Salt andpepper to taste
- For the lemon and parsley sauce:
- 1/4 cup of gluten-free mayonnaise
- Juice of 1 lemon
- Fresh parsley, chopped
- Salt and pepper to taste

DIRECTIONS:

1. Preheat the grill to medium-high heat.
2. In a small bowl, mix together the mayonnaise, lemon juice, chopped parsley, salt, and pepper. Set aside.
3. Season the salmon fillets with lemon juice, olive oil, garlic, salt, and pepper.
4. Grill the salmon for about 6 minutes per side, or until the salmon is cooked and flakes easily with a fork.
5. Serve the grilled salmon with the lemon and parsley sauce on top. Garnish with a bit of chopped fresh parsley.

NUTRITIONS:

Calories 300, Carbohydrates 2g, Fats 22g, Proteins 24g, Fiber 0g, Sugars 1g.

TIPS:

For an elegant dinner option, give grilled salmon with lemon and parsley sauce a go! The light yet flavorful dish pairs perfectly with steamed veggies or mixed greens for all-round goodness. Don't forget to check that the mayo used is gluten free too - no need to compromise on taste here!

GRILLED BEEF STEAK WITH ROASTED VEGETABLE SIDE

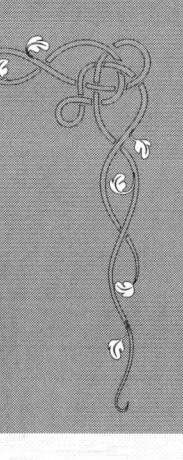

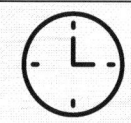

Prep time: 15 minutes

Cooking Time: 20 minutes

Servings: 4

INGREDIENTS:

- 4 beef steaks (about 7 oz. each)
- 2 tablespoons of olive oil
- 2 cloves of garlic, chopped
- 1 teaspoon of dried oregano
- Salt and pepper to taste
- For the roasted vegetable side:
- 2 zucchinis, cut into rounds
- 2 bell peppers (red and yellow), cut into strips
- 1 red onion, cut into wedges
- 1 tablespoon of olive oil
- Salt and pepper to taste
- Fresh rosemary, chopped, for garnish

DIRECTIONS:

1. Preheat the grill or a pan over medium-high heat.
2. Season the beef steaks with olive oil, garlic, oregano, salt, and pepper.
3. Grill the steaks for about 3-5 minutes per side, or until desired doneness is reached.
4. While the steaks are cooking, prepare the roasted vegetable side. On a baking sheet, spread out the zucchinis, bell peppers, and onion. Season with olive oil, salt, and pepper.
5. Cook the vegetables in a preheated oven at 425°F (220°C) for about 15 minutes, or until they are tender and slightly golden.
6. Serve the grilled beef steaks accompanied by the roasted vegetable side. Garnish with chopped fresh rosemary.

NUTRITIONS:

Calories 350, Carbohydrates 10g, Fats 20g, Proteins 35g, Fiber 3g, Sugars 5g.

TIPS:

Craving something hearty? Get grilling those beef steaks served up with roasted veggie sides - this classic meat combo will leave everyone feeling satisfied come dinnertime! Adjust doneness according to personal preference.

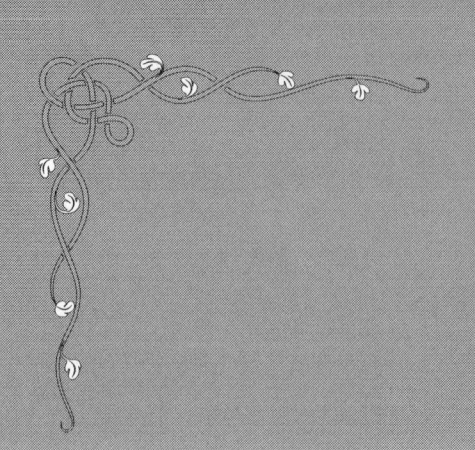

BEEF CHILI

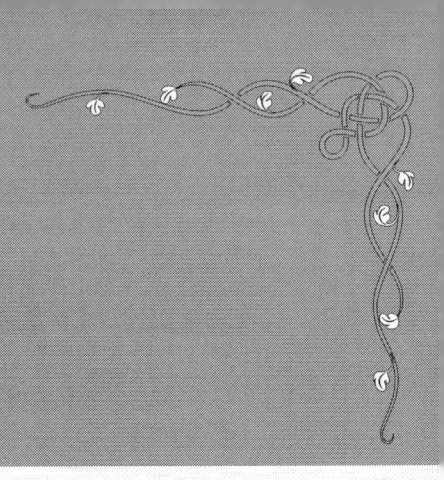

Prep time: 15 minutes

Cooking Time: 90 minutes

Servings: 4-6

INGREDIENTS:

- 7 oz. of ground beef
- 1 onion, chopped
- 2 cloves of garlic, chopped
- 1 red bell pepper, diced
- 1 green bell pepper, diced
- 1 can of red beans, drained and rinsed
- 1 can of black beans, drained and rinsed
- 1 can of diced tomatoes
- 2 tablespoons of tomato paste
- 1 cup of gluten-free beef broth
- 1 teaspoon of chili powder (or more, depending on the desired level of spiciness)
- 1 teaspoon of cumin powder
- Salt and pepper to taste
- Olive oil for cooking
- Fresh coriander, chopped, for garnish (optional)
- Gluten-free cheddar cheese flakes, for garnish (optional)
- Gluten-free sour cream, for garnish (optional)

NUTRITIONS:

Calories 350, Carbohydrates 30g, Fats 15g, Proteins 25g, Fiber 8g, Sugars 4g.

DIRECTIONS:

1. In a large pot or casserole, heat a bit of olive oil over medium heat. Add the onion and garlic and cook until they are translucent and fragrant.
2. Add the ground beef and cook until it is well browned and cooked.
3. Add the diced bell peppers and cook for a few minutes until they soften slightly.
4. Add the red beans, black beans, diced tomatoes, tomato paste, beef broth, chili powder, cumin, salt, and pepper. Stir well.
5. Bring the chili to a boil, then reduce the heat and let it simmer for at least 1 hour, covered, stirring occasionally.
6. Taste and adjust the seasonings if necessary.
7. Serve the hot chili, garnishing with chopped fresh coriander, cheddar cheese flakes, and a dollop of sour cream (if desired).

TIPS:

Serve it alone or with accompaniments like white rice, nachos, gluten-free cornbread - all of which can be topped off with sliced avocado, pickled jalapenos or chopped green onions for an added kick.

Snack & Appetizers

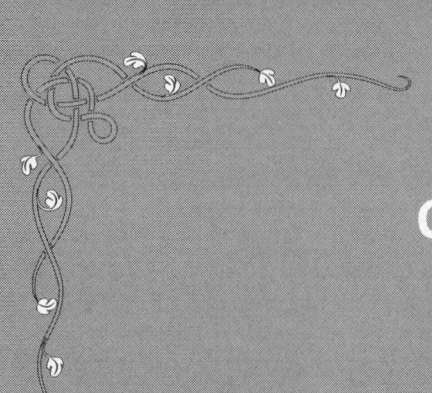

CRISPY ZUCCHINI STICKS

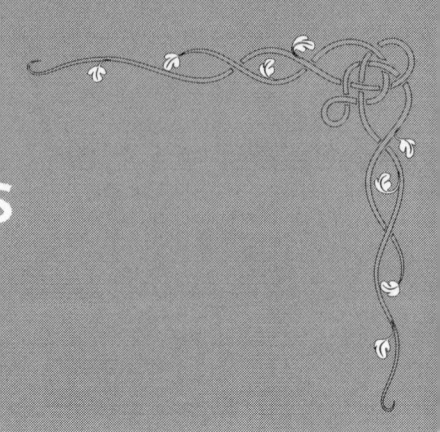

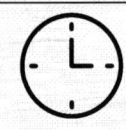

Prep time: 15 minutes

Cooking Time: 25 minutes

Servings: 4

INGREDIENTS:

- 2 medium zucchinis
- 1 cup of rice flour
- 2 eggs
- 1 cup of gluten-free breadcrumbs
- 1/2 teaspoon of salt
- 1/2 teaspoon of pepper
- 1/2 teaspoon of garlic powder
- Marinara sauce for serving

DIRECTIONS:

1. Preheat the oven to 425°F (220°C) and line a baking sheet with parchment paper.
2. Cut the zucchinis into sticks about 1/2 inch thick.
3. In three separate bowls, put the rice flour, beaten eggs, and breadcrumbs mixed with salt, pepper, and garlic powder.
4. Dip each zucchini stick first in the flour, then in the egg, and finally in the breadcrumbs, making sure it is well covered.
5. Arrange the zucchini sticks on the baking sheet and bake for 25 minutes or until they become golden and crispy.
6. Serve hot with marinara sauce.

NUTRITIONS:

Calories: 180, Fats: 3g, Carbohydrates: 32g, Proteins: 6g, Fiber: 2g, Sugars: 4g

TIPS:

try adding grated parmesan to the breadcrumbs for extra flavor.

BEET HUMMUS

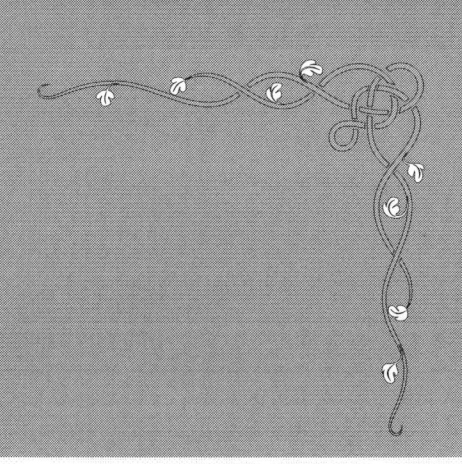

Prep time: 10 minutes

Cooking Time: 0 minutes

Servings: 6

INGREDIENTS:

- 1 cooked beet, cut into cubes
- 1 can of chickpeas, drained and rinsed
- 2 cloves of garlic
- 2 tablespoons of tahini
- Juice of 1 lemon
- 3 tablespoons of olive oil
- Salt and pepper to taste
- Raw vegetables for serving

DIRECTIONS:

1. In a blender or food processor, add the beet, chickpeas, garlic, tahini, lemon juice, and olive oil.
2. Blend until you get a smooth and creamy consistency. Add salt and pepper to taste.
3. Serve the hummus with raw vegetables such as carrots, cucumbers, or bell peppers.

NUTRITIONS:

Calories: 150, Fats: 8g, Carbohydrates: 16g, Proteins: 5g, Fiber: 4g, Sugars: 3g

TIPS:

If you're looking for something more liquid then add a little water or olive oil to your mix! This irresistible dish is perfect as leftovers too; store it in the fridge and reheat when needed.

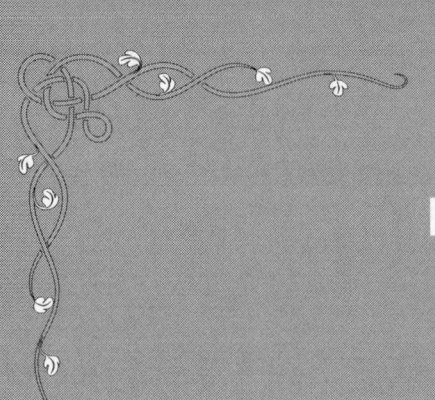

MINI EGGPLANT PIZZAS

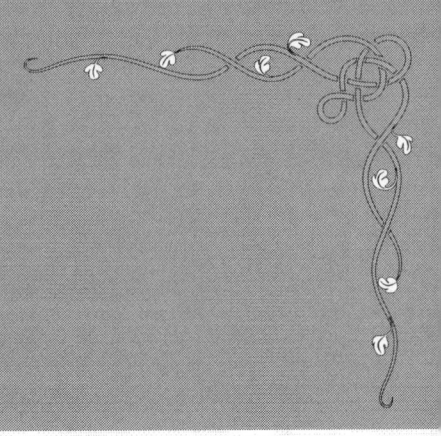

Prep time: 15 minutes

Cooking Time: 20 minutes

Servings: 4

INGREDIENTS:

- 1 large eggplant
- 1 cup of tomato sauce
- 1 cup of grated mozzarella
- 1/2 cup of fresh basil
- Salt and pepper to taste
- Olive oil

DIRECTIONS:

1. Preheat the oven to 400°F (200°C) and line a baking sheet with parchment paper.
2. Cut the eggplant into slices about 1/2 inch thick.
3. Arrange the eggplant slices on the baking sheet, sprinkle with a bit of salt and pepper and a drizzle of olive oil.
4. Bake in the oven for 10 minutes.
5. Remove the baking sheet from the oven, top each eggplant slice with the tomato sauce and grated mozzarella.
6. Put back in the oven and bake for another 10 minutesor until the cheese has melted and browned.
7. Garnish with fresh basil before serving.

NUTRITIONS:

Calories: 140, Fats: 7g, Carbohydrates: 13g, Proteins: 7g, Fiber: 4g, Sugars: 6g

TIPS:

You can be more creative by adding ingredients like olives, bell peppers and mushrooms.

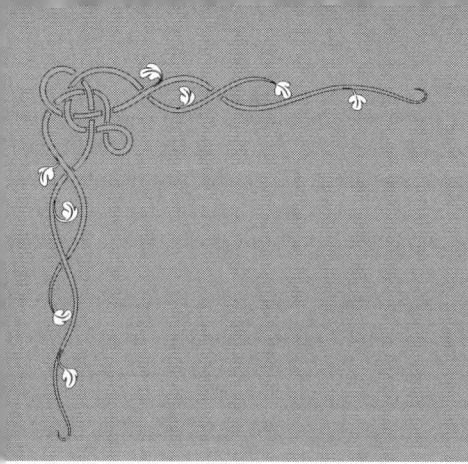

BAKED KALE CHIPS

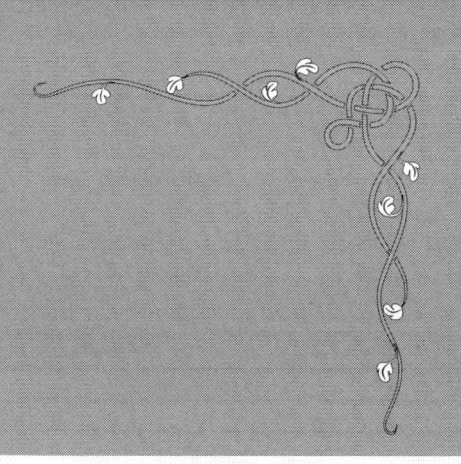

Prep time: 10 minutes

Cooking Time: 15 minutes

Servings: 4

INGREDIENTS:
- 1 bunch of kale
- 1 tablespoon of olive oil
- Salt and pepper to taste

DIRECTIONS:
1. Preheat the oven to 300°F (150°C) and line a baking sheet with parchment paper.
2. Remove the kale leaves from the stem and cut them into bite-sized pieces.
3. Put the kale leaves in a large bowl, add the olive oil and a pinch of salt and pepper. Mix well to ensure all the leaves are lightly coated.
4. Arrange the kale leaves on the baking sheet in a single layer.
5. Bake in the oven for 10-15 minutes or until the edges of the leaves start to turn brown.
6. Let cool before serving.

NUTRITIONS:
Calories: 58, Fats: 3.5g, Carbohydrates: 7g, Proteins: 2g, Fiber: 1g, Sugars: 0g

TIPS:
they can also be sprinkled over salads or soups to add a delightful crunch. Make sure not to overcook them though - you don't want your delicious treat turning bitter!

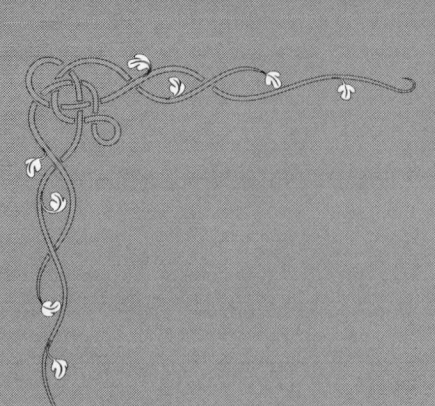

QUINOA AND SPINACH MEATBALLS

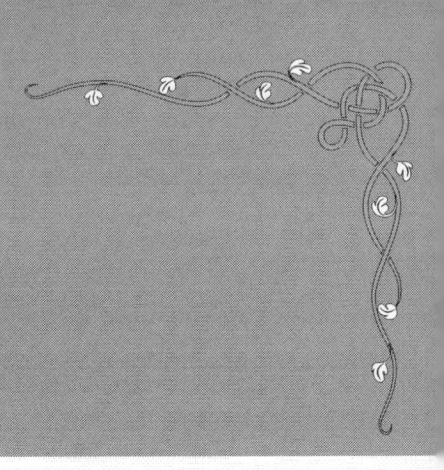

Prep time: 20 minutes

Cooking Time: 20 minutes

Servings: 4

INGREDIENTS:

- 1 cup of cooked quinoa
- 2 cups of fresh spinach
- 1 egg
- 1/2 cup of crumbled feta cheese
- Salt and pepper to taste
- Olive oil

DIRECTIONS:

1. Preheat the oven to 375°F (190°C) and line a baking sheet with parchment paper.
2. In a large bowl, combine the cooked quinoa, chopped spinach, egg, and feta cheese. Season with salt and pepper to taste.
3. Form small meatballs with the mixture and arrange them on the baking sheet.
4. Bake in the oven for 20 minutes or until the meatballs become golden.
5. Serve hot.

NUTRITIONS:

Calories: 210, Fats: 8g, Carbohydrates: 26g, Proteins: 9g, Fiber: 3g, Sugars: 2g

TIPS:

Meatballs pair perfectly with a creamy yogurt sauce, or make for the perfect side dish when served alongside veggies and/or salad.

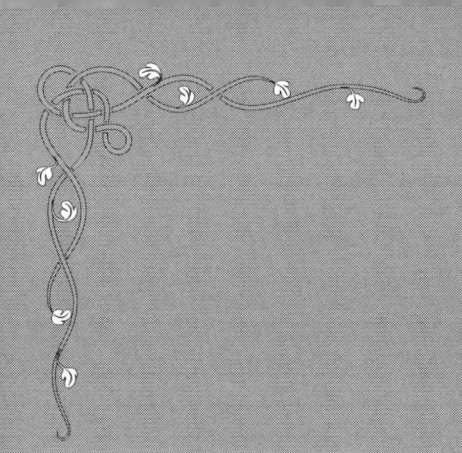

TOMATO AND BASIL BRUSCHETTA

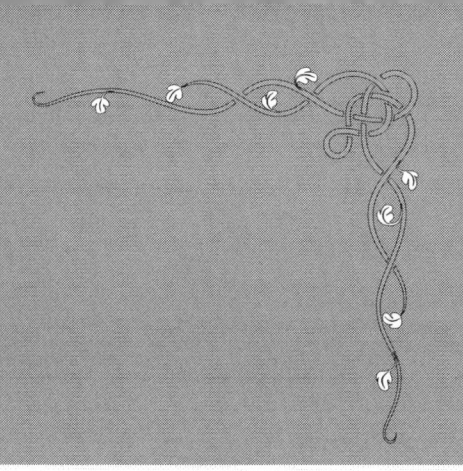

Prep time: 10 minutes

Cooking Time: 5 minutes

Servings: 4

INGREDIENTS:

- 1 gluten-free baguette
- 2 ripe tomatoes
- 1 bunch of fresh basil
- 2 cloves of garlic
- 3 tablespoons of olive oil
- Salt and pepper to taste

DIRECTIONS:

1. Preheat the oven to 350°F (175°C).
2. Cut the gluten-free baguette into slices about 1/2 inch thick and arrange them on a baking sheet.
3. Bake in the oven for 5 minutes or until the slices become slightly toasted.
4. In the meantime, cut the tomatoes into cubes and chop the basil.
5. In a bowl, combine the tomatoes, basil, olive oil, and a pinch of salt and pepper.
6. Rub each slice of bread with a clove of garlic, then top with the tomato and basil mix.
7. Serve immediately.

NUTRITIONS:

Calories: 180, Fats: 7g, Carbohydrates: 26g, Proteins: 4g, Fiber: 2g, Sugars: 3g

TIPS:

For bruschetta night, why not step it up a notch by adding some fresh mozzarella or goat cheese before serving?

SWEET POTATO CROSTINI WITH AVOCADO AND SMOKED SALMON

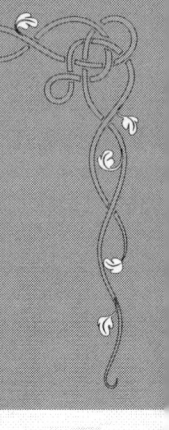

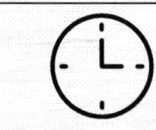

Prep time: 15 minutes

Cooking Time: 20 minutes

Servings: 4

INGREDIENTS:

- 2 medium sweet potatoes
- 1 ripe avocado
- 0,4 lb. of smoked salmon
- Juice of 1 lemon
- Salt and pepper to taste
- Olive oil

DIRECTIONS:

1. Preheat the oven to 400°F (200°C) and cover a baking sheet with parchment paper for optimal results.
2. Slice up your sweet potatoes into 1/2 inch thick pieces, then place them on the tray and drizzle some olive oil over top along with light sprinkling of salt.
3. Pop it in the oven for 20 minutes or until they reach desired level of tenderness.
4. Meanwhile, mash up that avocado in a bowl - make sure to add lemon juice, some salt & pepper to taste!
5. Once your sweet potato slices are ready they'll be perfect for topping off with mashed avocado and smoked salmon - serve right away and enjoy!

NUTRITIONS:

Calories: 220, Fats: 11g, Carbohydrates: 22g, Proteins: 10g, Fiber: 5g, Sugars: 5g

TIPS:

These crostini are a great appetizer or snack. You can also add a bit of fresh dill or sesame seeds for extra flavor.

VEGETABLE SPRING ROLLS

Prep time: 30 minutes

Cooking Time: 0 minutes

Servings: 4

INGREDIENTS:

- 8 rice sheets (8 inch)
- 2 carrots
- 1 cucumber
- 1 red pepper
- 1 bunch of fresh mint
- Gluten-free soy sauce for serving

DIRECTIONS:

1. Start by cutting the carrots, cucumber and pepper into thin strips.
2. Then take one rice sheet at a time and dip it in warm water for just a few seconds until it's soft enough to lay on your plate.
3. Now pile up some of the carrot pieces, add some crunchy cucumber slices as well as colorful peppers - feel free to throw in some fresh mint leaves too if you like!
4. Carefully roll everything together making sure to fold both sides inward so that your spring rolls are nice and sealed. Continue doing this with all the other sheets until all your veggies have been used up
5. Serve the spring rolls with the gluten-free soy sauce.

NUTRITIONS:

Calories: 120, Fats: 0g, Carbohydrates: 28g, Proteins: 2g, Fiber: 2g, Sugars: 3g

TIPS:

When working with rice sheets, make sure to have a bowl of warm water on hand to soften them. Dip one sheet at a time for a few seconds, then lay it on a plate and fill it with your preferred filling. Remember that rice sheets can become sticky when wet, so try to work quickly once you've dipped them in water.

SWEET POTATO NACHOS

Prep time: 15 minutes

Cooking Time: 30 minutes

Servings: 4

INGREDIENTS:

- 2 large sweet potatoes
- 1 cup of black beans, drained and rinsed
- 1 cup of corn
- 1 cup of grated cheddar cheese
- 1 avocado, cut into cubes
- Salsa, sour cream, and fresh cilantro for serving

NUTRITIONS:

Calories: 320, Fats: 14g, Carbohydrates: 40g, Proteins: 10g, Fiber: 7g, Sugars: 8g

TIPS:

To get super crispy sweet potatoes, cut them into thin slices and bake in a single layer. If the pieces are overlapping, they will steam instead of crisping up - so make sure to spread them out as much as possible!

DIRECTIONS:

1. Preheat the oven to 400°F (200°C) and line a baking sheet with parchment paper.
2. Cut the sweet potatoes into thin slices and arrange them on the baking sheet in a single layer.
3. Bake in the oven for 15 minutes, then flip the slices and bake for another 15 minutes or until they become crispy.
4. Remove the baking sheet from the oven and top the sweet potatoes with the black beans, corn, and cheddar cheese.
5. Put it back in the oven and bake for another 5 minutes or until the cheese has melted.
6. Serve the sweet potato nachos with the avocado, salsa, sour cream, and fresh cilantro.

SHRIMP AND PINEAPPLE SKEWERS

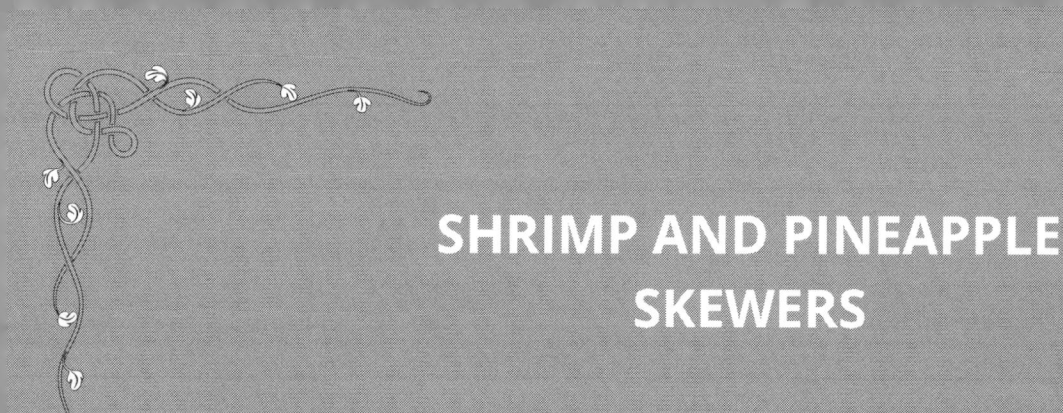

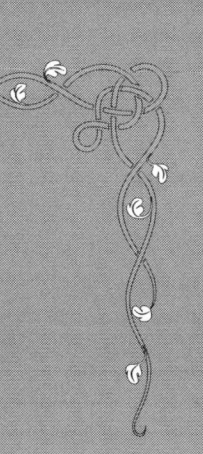

Prep time: 20 minutes

Cooking Time: 10 minutes

Servings: 4

INGREDIENTS:

- 1lb of shrimp, peeled and cleaned
- 1 fresh pineapple
- 2 red peppers
- 2 tablespoons of olive oil
- Salt and pepper to taste
- Gluten-free teriyaki sauce for serving

DIRECTIONS:

1. Preheat the grill or barbecue to medium-high heat.
2. Cut the pineapple and peppers into pieces similar in size to the shrimp.
3. Skewer the shrimp, pineapple, and peppers on skewers, alternating the pieces.
4. Brush the skewers with olive oil and season with salt and pepper.
5. Grill the skewers for 2-3 minutes per side, or until the shrimp turn pink and the pineapple and peppers start to caramelize.
6. Serve the shrimp and pineapple skewers with the gluten-free teriyaki sauce.

NUTRITIONS:

Calories: 220, Fats: 6g, Carbohydrates: 20g, Proteins: 24g, Fiber: 2g, Sugars: 15g

TIPS:

For shrimp on the grill, don't overcook or you'll end up with rubbery bites. Soak wooden skewers for at least 20 minutes before grilling to keep them from burning too quickly. Also you cane marinade the shrimp in some gluten-free teriyaki sauce if you want an extra zing of flavor.

CHICKEN AND ZUCCHINI MEATBALLS

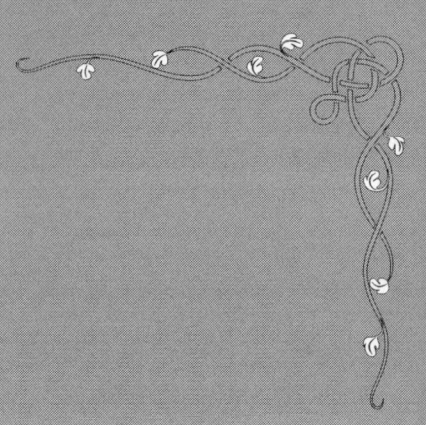

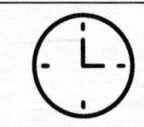

Prep time: 20 minutes

Cooking Time: 25 minutes

Servings: 4

INGREDIENTS:

- 1 lb of ground chicken breast
- 2 medium zucchinis, grated
- 1 egg
- 1/4 cup of gluten-free breadcrumbs
- 2 tablespoons of grated Parmesan cheese
- 1 clove of garlic, minced
- 1 tablespoon of fresh parsley, minced
- Salt and pepper to taste
- Olive oil

NUTRITIONS:

Calories: 240, Fats: 10g, Carbohydrates: 7g, Proteins: 29g, Fiber: 1g, Sugars: 2g

TIPS:

Get creative when it comes to making meatballs - add spices like turmeric, cumin or paprika for a tasty bite! You can also prep ahead of time and just reheat when ready serve (perfect appetizer).

DIRECTIONS:

1. In a large bowl, combine the ground chicken breast, grated zucchini, egg, gluten-free breadcrumbs, Parmesan cheese, minced garlic, and parsley.
2. Season with salt and pepper to taste and mix well to combine all the ingredients.
3. Take a portion of the mixture and form uniform-sized meatballs.
4. Heat a bit of olive oil in a non-stick pan over medium-high heat.
5. Add the meatballs to the pan and cook for about 4-5 minutes per side or until they are well cooked and golden.
6. Drain them on paper towels to remove excess oil.
7. Serve the chicken and zucchini meatballs hot with a side sauce of your choice.

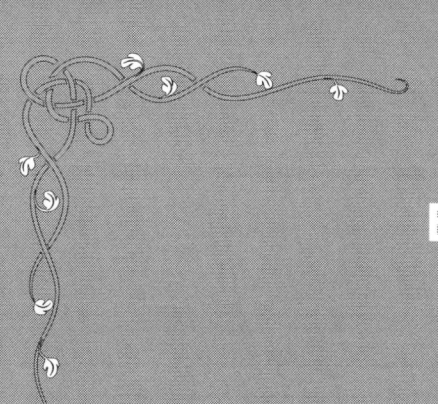

BAKED ZUCCHINI CHIPS

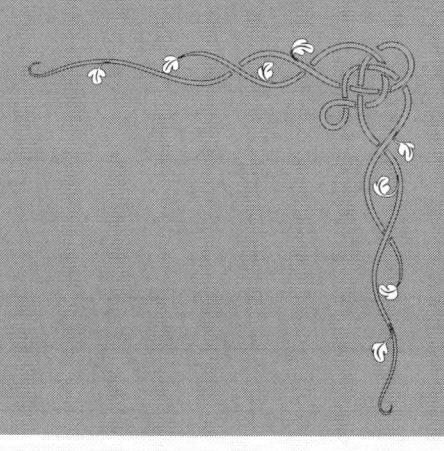

Prep time: 10 minutes

Cooking Time: 25 minutes

Servings: 4

INGREDIENTS:
- 2 medium zucchinis
- 2 tablespoons of olive oil
- 1/2 teaspoon of paprika
- 1/2 teaspoon of garlic powder
- Salt and pepper to taste

DIRECTIONS:
1. Preheat the oven to 400°F (200°C) and line a baking sheet with parchment paper.
2. Cut the zucchinis into thin slices, about 1/4 inch thick.
3. In a bowl, mix together the olive oil, paprika, garlic powder, salt, and pepper.
4. Dip the zucchini slices in the seasoning mixture to coat them evenly.
5. Arrange the zucchini slices on the baking sheet in a single layer.
6. Bake the zucchini chips in the oven for about 20-25 minutes or until they become crispy and slightly golden.
7. Remove the zucchini chips from the oven and let them cool slightly before serving.

NUTRITIONS:
Calories: 70, Fats: 5g, Carbohydrates: 5g, Proteins: 2g, Fiber: 1g, Sugars: 3g

TIPS:
step up your game with zucchini chips by adding chili powder, cumin or dried parsley – plus marinating the slices in olive oil & spices for 15-30 minutes beforehand gives an intense flavor that's hard to beat. Enjoy these delicious snacks solo or pair with a light dip.

Dessert

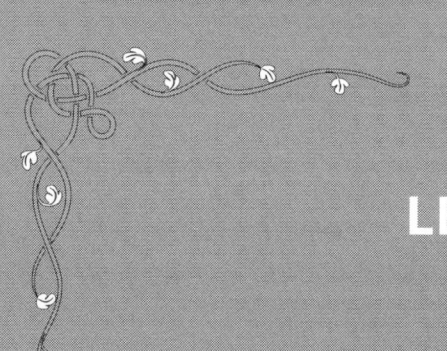

LEMON AND POPPY SEED MUFFINS

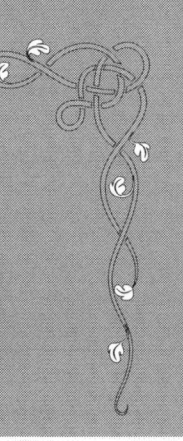

Prep time: 20 minutes

Cooking Time: 15 minutes

Servings: 12 Muffins

INGREDIENTS:

- 2 cups of gluten-free flour mix
- 1 cup of sugar
- 2 teaspoons of baking powder
- 1/2 teaspoon of salt
- 1 tablespoon of poppy seeds
- Grated zest of 1 lemon
- 3/4 cup of lactose-free milk
- 1/2 cup of sunflower seed oil
- 2 large eggs
- 1 teaspoon of vanilla extract

DIRECTIONS:

1. Preheat the oven to 375°F (190°C) and prepare a muffin tin with 12 paper liners.
2. In a large bowl, mix the flour, sugar, baking powder, salt, poppy seeds, and lemon zest.
3. In another bowl, mix the milk, oil, eggs, and vanilla extract. Add these wet ingredients to the dry ingredients and stir until just combined.
4. Distribute the batter into the liners and bake for 20-25 minutes, or until a toothpick inserted in the center comes out clean.
5. Let the muffins cool in the tin for 5 minutes, then transfer them to a rack to cool completely.

NUTRITIONS:

Calories: 280, Fats: 14g, Carbohydrates: 36g, Proteins: 6g, Fiber: 4g, Sugars: 18g.

TIPS:

For an extra special touch, sprinkle the muffins with a dusting of powdered sugar before serving. Let them cool completely to enjoy their best texture - and for a truly intense lemon flavor, add some freshly squeezed juice into the batter.

APPLE CAKE

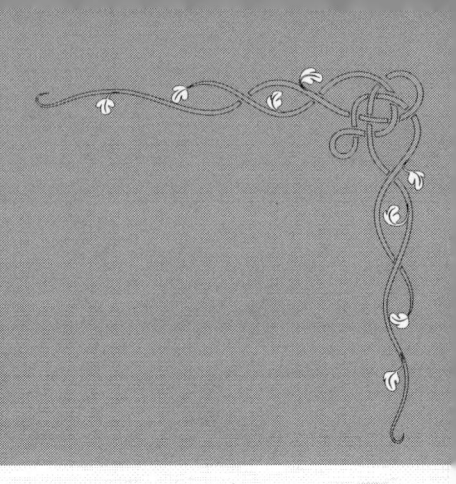

Prep time: 20 minutes

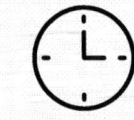

Cooking Time: 50 minutes

Servings: 8

INGREDIENTS:

- 2 cups of gluten-free flour mix
- 1 cup of sugar
- 2 teaspoons of baking powder
- 1/2 teaspoon of salt
- 1 teaspoon of cinnamon
- 1/2 teaspoon of nutmeg
- 1/2 cup of sunflower seed oil
- 2 large eggs
- 1/4 cup of lactose-free milk
- 1 teaspoon of vanilla extract
- 2 large apples, peeled, cored, and thinly sliced

NUTRITIONS:

Calories: 320, Fats: 15g, Carbohydrates: 42g, Proteins: 5g, Fiber: 3g, Sugars: 22g

TIPS:

For an extra special touch, try sprinkling your cake with a dusting of powdered sugar before serving. Make the texture even more interesting by incorporating different varieties of apples - for example, tart Granny Smith or sweet Honeycrisp. To keep the fruit juicy and succulent during preparation, simply submerge them in a bowl filled with cold water and lemon juice!

DIRECTIONS:

1. Preheat your oven to 350°F (175°C) and give a 9-inch cake pan a nice, thorough greasing.
2. Now grab a big bowl and mix together the flour, sugar, baking powder, salt, cinnamon and nutmeg.
3. In another bowl whisk together the oil with eggs followed by milk plus vanilla extract then add this wet mixture into your dry ingredients until just barely mixed. Carefully fold the apple slices into the batter.
4. Pour the batter into the prepared pan and level the surface with a spatula. Bake for 50-60 minutes or until when you poke through with of toothpick comes out cleanish.
5. Let cool within its confines on wire rack for 10 minutes before transferring onto plate/board thingy - now let cool completely before serving up this delicious delight!

CHOCOLATE COOKIES

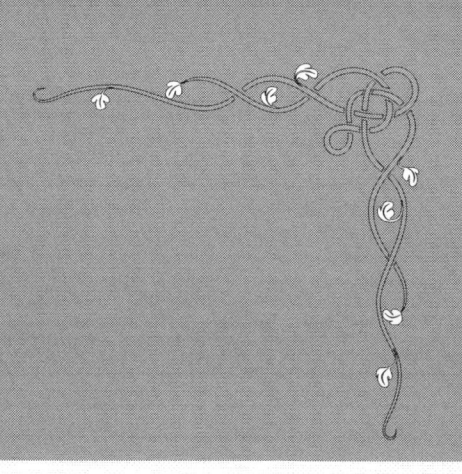

Prep time: 15 minutes

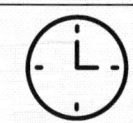

Cooking Time: 12 minutes

Servings: 24 Cookies

INGREDIENTS:

- 2 cups of gluten-free flour mix
- 1/2 cup of unsweetened cocoa powder
- 1 teaspoon of baking soda
- 1/2 teaspoon of salt
- 1 cup of sugar
- 1/2 cup of lactose-free butter, softened
- 2 large eggs
- 1 teaspoon of vanilla extract
- 1 cup of gluten-free chocolate chips

NUTRITIONS:

Calories: 150, Fats: 7g, Carbohydrates: 20g, Proteins: 3g, Fiber: 2g, Sugars: 12g

TIPS:

As an alternative to chocolate chips, add some crunchy chopped nuts or dried fruits into your cookie batter; just be sure not to overbake them in order to get that soft-and-chewy consistency.

DIRECTIONS:

1. Preheat the oven to 350°F (175°C) and line two baking sheets with parchment paper.
2. In a medium bowl, combine the flour, cocoa powder, baking soda, and salt.
3. In a large bowl, mix the sugar and butter until creamy. Add the eggs, one at a time, mixing well after each addition. Add the vanilla extract.
4. Gradually add the flour mixture to the butter mixture, stirring just until the ingredients come together. Add the chocolate chips and gently mix.
5. With a spoon, form mounds of dough and place them on the baking sheet, leaving about 2 inches of space between each cookie.
6. Bake for 10-12 minutes, or until the edges are set but the center is still soft. Let the cookies cool on the baking sheets for 5 minutes, then transfer them to a rack to cool completely.

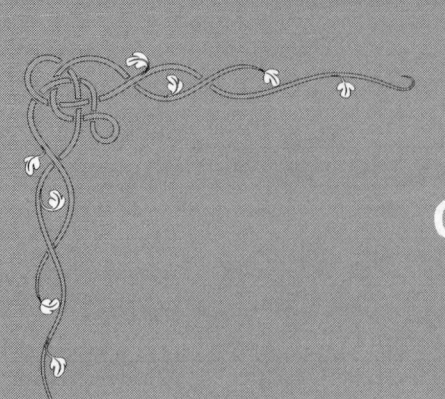

CHOCOLATE BROWNIES

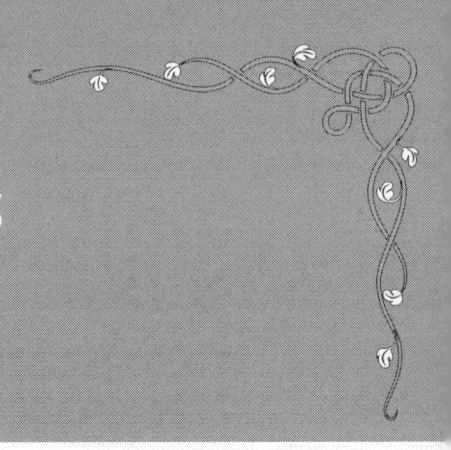

Prep time: 20 minutes

Cooking Time: 35 minutes

Servings: 16

INGREDIENTS:

- 1 cup of gluten-free flour mix
- 1/2 cup of unsweetened cocoa powder
- 1/2 teaspoon of salt
- 1 cup of sugar
- 1/2 cup of lactose-free butter, melted
- 3 large eggs
- 1 teaspoon of vanilla extract
- 1 cup of gluten-free chocolate chips

DIRECTIONS:

1. Preheat the oven to 350°F (175°C) and line an 8x8 inch baking pan with parchment paper.
2. In a medium bowl, combine the flour, cocoa powder, and salt.
3. In a large bowl, mix the sugar and melted butter. Add the eggs, one at a time, mixing well after each addition. Add the vanilla extract.
4. Gradually add the flour mixture to the butter mixture, stirring just until the ingredients come together. Add the chocolate chips and gently mix.
5. Pour the batter into the prepared pan and level the surface with a spatula.
6. Bake for 30-35 minutes, or until a toothpick inserted in the center comes out with a few crumbs attached. Let the brownies cool completely in the pan on a rack.
7. Once cooled, cut the brownies into about 2-inch squares.

NUTRITIONS:

Calories: 180, Fats: 9g, Carbohydrates: 24g, Proteins: 3g, Fiber: 2g, Sugars: 16g.

TIPS:

For an extra special touch, sprinkle your brownies with a dusting of powdered sugar before serving. If you're looking for something more dense and fudgy, extend the baking time by a few minutes - just make sure to keep an eye on them since they'll continue to bake even after being taken out of the oven. Another tip is to use a sharp, clean knife to cut the brownies: this will help you get cleaner edges.

BANANA PANCAKES

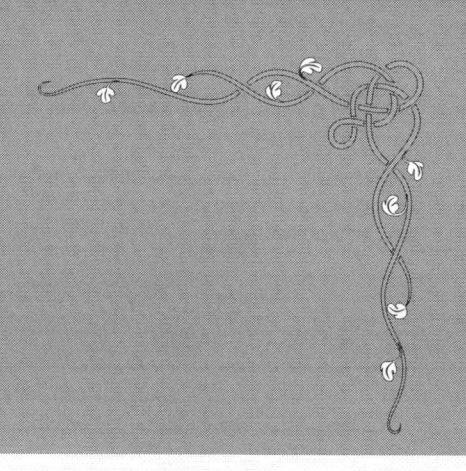

| Prep time: 10 minutes | Cooking Time: 15 minutes | Servings: 4 |

INGREDIENTS:

- 1 cup of gluten-free flour mix
- 1 tablespoon of sugar
- 1/2 teaspoon of baking soda
- 1/2 teaspoon of salt
- 1 ripe banana, mashed
- 1 cup of lactose-free milk
- 1 large egg
- 1 teaspoon of vanilla extract
- Oil for cooking

DIRECTIONS:

1. In a medium bowl, combine the flour, sugar, baking soda, and salt.
2. In another bowl, mix the mashed banana, milk, egg, and vanilla extract.
3. Add the banana mixture to the flour mixture, stirring just until the ingredients come together.
4. Heat a bit of oil in a non-stick pan over medium heat. Pour about 1/4 cup of batter for each pancake into the pan and cook until bubbles form on the surface, then flip it and cook on the other side.
5. Serve the pancakes hot with maple syrup, fresh fruit, or chopped nuts.

NUTRITIONS:

Calories: 210, Fats: 4g, Carbohydrates: 40g, Proteins: 6g, Fiber: 3g, Sugars: 12g.

TIPS:

For added flavor complexity, consider adding some spices like cinnamon or nutmeg into the flour mixture while preparing these gooey treats. If you prefer fluffier pancakes, try cooking them at a lower heat for a longer time.

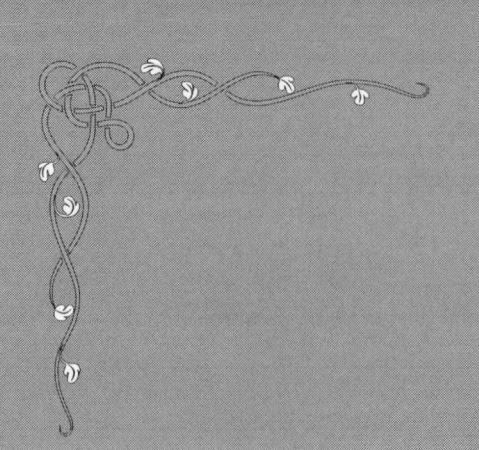

CARROT CAKE

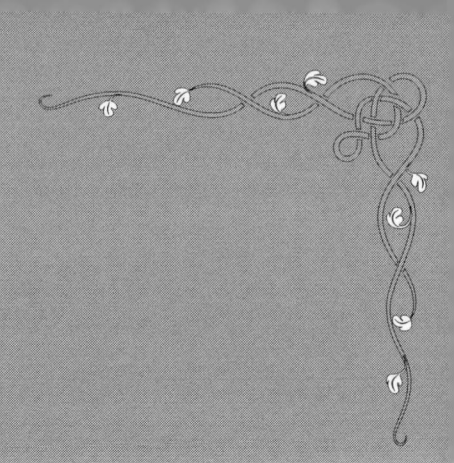

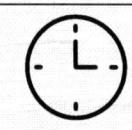

Prep time: 20 minutes

Cooking Time: 40 minutes

Servings: 12

INGREDIENTS:

- 2 cups of gluten-free flour mix
- 2 teaspoons of baking powder
- 1/2 teaspoon of baking soda
- 1/2 teaspoon of salt
- 1 teaspoon of cinnamon
- 1/2 teaspoon of nutmeg
- 1 cup of sugar
- 1/2 cup of sunflower seed oil
- 4 large eggs
- 2 cups of grated carrots
- 1 cup of chopped nuts (optional)

NUTRITIONS:

Calories: 280, Fats: 12g, Carbohydrates: 38g, Proteins: 6g, Fiber: 3g, Sugars: 20g

TIPS:

For a delectable finish, give your cake the perfect touch by dusting it with powdered sugar. If you like an extra moist texture, cut back on baking time; the residual heat will keep cooking even after it's pulled from the oven. For freshness and added flavor, use carrots you freshly grate yourself instead of pre-packaged ones!

DIRECTIONS:

1. Preheat the oven to 350°F (175°C) and grease a 9x13 inch baking pan.
2. In a medium bowl, combine the flour, baking powder, baking soda, salt, cinnamon, and nutmeg.
3. In a large bowl, mix the sugar and oil. Add the eggs, one at a time, mixing well after each addition.
4. Gradually add the flour mixture to the egg mixture, stirring just until the ingredients come together. Add the grated carrots and chopped nuts, if using, and gently mix.
5. Pour the batter into the prepared pan and level the surface with a spatula.
6. Bake for 35-40 minutes, or until a toothpick inserted in the center comes out clean. Let the cake cool completely in the pan on a rack.

LOW-SUGAR PUMPKIN MUFFINS

Prep time: 15 minutes

Cooking Time: 20 minutes

Servings: 12 Muffins

INGREDIENTS:

- 2 cups of gluten-free flour mix
- 1 tablespoon of cinnamon
- 1 teaspoon of nutmeg
- 1/2 teaspoon of cloves
- 2 teaspoons of baking powder
- 1/2 teaspoon of baking soda
- 1/2 teaspoon of salt
- 1/2 cup of sweetener (such as stevia or erythritol)
- 1 cup of pumpkin puree
- 1/2 cup of sunflower seed oil
- 2 large eggs
- 1 teaspoon of vanilla extract

DIRECTIONS:

1. Preheat the oven to 375°F (190°C) and prepare a muffin tin with 12 paper liners.
2. In a large bowl, combine the flour, cinnamon, nutmeg, cloves, baking powder, baking soda, salt, and sweetener.
3. In another bowl, mix the pumpkin puree, oil, eggs, and vanilla extract.
4. Add the pumpkin mixture to the flour mixture, stirring just until the ingredients come together.
5. Distribute the batter among the liners and bake for 20-25 minutes, or until a toothpick inserted in the center comes out clean.
6. Let the muffins cool in the tin for 5 minutes, then transfer them to a rack to cool completely.

NUTRITIONS:

Calories: 180, Fats: 10g, Carbohydrates: 20g, Proteins: 4g, Fiber: 3g, Sugars: 4g

TIPS:

For a truly special finish, sprinkle the muffins with pumpkin seeds before popping them in the oven. To ensure that perfect texture, wait for them to cool completely before indulging!

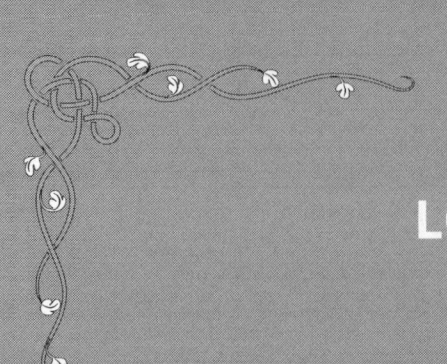

LOW-SUGAR CHOCOLATE PUDDING

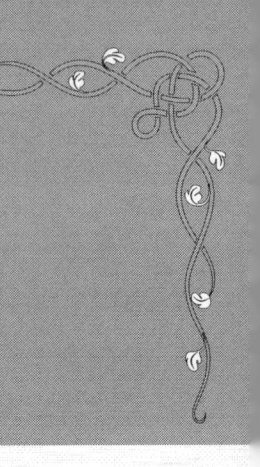

Prep time: 10 minutes	Cooking Time: 10 minutes	Servings: 4

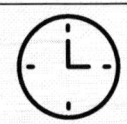

INGREDIENTS:

- 2 cups of lactose-free milk
- 3 tablespoons of unsweetened cocoa powder
- 2 tablespoons of cornstarch
- 1/4 cup of sweetener (such as stevia or erythritol)
- 1 teaspoon of vanilla extract
- 1 pinch of salt

DIRECTIONS:

1. Heat up a medium saucepan and whisk together the milk, cocoa powder, cornstarch, sweetener and salt.
2. Increase the heat until it starts to boil then reduce it to low-medium. Stir constantly for 2-3 minutes or until you see that the pudding has thickened.
3. Take off of heat and mix in vanilla extract.
4. Divide among 4 bowls evenly before letting cool at room temperature for about 10 minutes before covering each bowl with plastic wrap and refrigerate for a minimum of two hours so that your pudding can fully set!

NUTRITIONS:

Calories: 110, Fats: 3g, Carbohydrates: 18g, Proteins: 4g, Fiber: 2g, Sugars: 4g

TIPS:

For an extra special touch, serve up this pudding with a dollop of sugar-free whipped cream and a light dusting of cocoa powder. Don't worry if it still seems too liquid when you take it off the heat—it will thicken as it cools.

CLASSIC SUGAR-FREE COOKIES

Prep time: 15 minutes	Cooking Time: 12-15 minutes	Servings: 24 Cookies

INGREDIENTS:

- 2 cups of gluten-free flour
- 1 teaspoon of baking powder
- 1/4 teaspoon of salt
- 1/2 cup of lactose-free butter, softened
- 1/2 cup of sweetener (such as stevia or erythritol)
- 2 large eggs
- 1 teaspoon of vanilla extract
- 1/2 cup of chopped nuts (optional)

NUTRITIONS:

Calories: 90, Fats: 6g, Carbohydrates: 7g, Proteins: 2g, Fiber: 1g, Sugars: 0g

TIPS:

For an extra touch, you can add sugar-free chocolate chips or spices like cinnamon or nutmeg to the dough. Remember, the cookies will harden slightly as they cool, so don't overbake them.

DIRECTIONS:

1. Preheat the oven to 350°F (175°C) and line a baking sheet with parchment paper.
2. In a medium bowl, combine the flour, baking powder, and salt.
3. In a large bowl, mix the butter and sweetener until creamy. Add the eggs, one at a time, mixing well after each addition. Add the vanilla extract.
4. Gradually add the flour mixture to the butter mixture, mixing just until the ingredients come together. Add the chopped nuts, if using, and gently mix.
5. Take small portions of dough and form small balls. Arrange the balls on the prepared baking sheet, leaving about 2 cm of space between the cookies.
6. Slightly flatten the cookies with the palm of your hand or the bottom of a glass.
7. Bake the cookies for 12-15 minutes, or until the edges are slightly golden.
8. Let the cookies cool on the baking sheet for a few minutes, then transfer them to a rack to cool completely.

SUGAR-FREE COCONUT PANNA COTTA

| Prep time: 10 minutes | Cooking Time: 10 minutes | Servings: 4 |

INGREDIENTS:

- 1 can (400 ml) of light coconut milk
- 1 cup of lactose-free cream
- 1/4 cup of sweetener (such as stevia or erythritol)
- 2 teaspoons of sugar-free powdered gelatin
- 1 teaspoon of vanilla extract

DIRECTIONS:

1. In a small bowl, mix the powdered gelatin with 1/4 cup of cold water and let it rest for 5 minutes.
2. In a pot, pour the coconut milk, cream, and sweetener. Heat the mixture over medium-low heat until it starts to boil.
3. Remove the pot from the heat and add the hydrated gelatin. Mix well until the gelatin completely dissolves.
4. Add the vanilla extract and mix again.
5. Pour the panna cotta mixture into 4 bowls or individual molds.
6. Let it cool at room temperature for a few minutes, then cover the bowls with plastic wrap and put them in the refrigerator for at least 2 hours, or until the panna cotta is completely cooled and set.

NUTRITIONS:

Calories: 160, Fats: 15g, Carbohydrates: 5g, Proteins:2g, Fiber: 0g, Sugars: 0g

TIPS:

When serving panna cotta for dessert, give it texture by topping with toasted coconut flakes or adding fresh fruit for that sweet but guilt-free taste. Plus, leaving the panna cotta in the refrigerator longer helps make sure everyone gets an even consistency in their portion.

STRAWBERRY CHEESECAKE

Prep time: 20 minutes

Cooking Time: 60 minutes

Servings: 8

INGREDIENTS:

- 2 cups of crushed gluten-free cookies
- 1/2 cup of unsalted butter, melted
- 3 8-ounce packages of cream cheese, softened
- 1 cup of sugar
- 1 teaspoon of vanilla extract
- 3 large eggs
- 1 cup of sour cream
- 1 cup of fresh strawberries, sliced

NUTRITIONS:

Calories: 450, Fats: 30g, Carbohydrates: 35g, Proteins: 8g, Fiber: 1g, Sugars: 25g

DIRECTIONS:

1. Preheat the oven to 325 degrees F (165 degrees C). In a medium bowl, mix the crushed cookies and melted butter. Press the mixture onto the bottom of a 9-inch cheesecake pan.
2. In a large bowl, mix the cream cheese, sugar, and vanilla extract until smooth. Add the eggs, one at a time, mixing well after each addition. Add the sour cream and mix until the mixture is smooth.
3. Pour the cream cheese mixture over the cookie crust. Level the surface with a spatula.
4. Bake in the preheated oven for 60 minutes, or until the center is almost set. Let it cool in the pan for 10 minutes, then remove the edge of the pan. Let it cool completely, then refrigerate for at least 3 hours before serving.
5. Before serving, garnish with fresh strawberries.

TIPS:

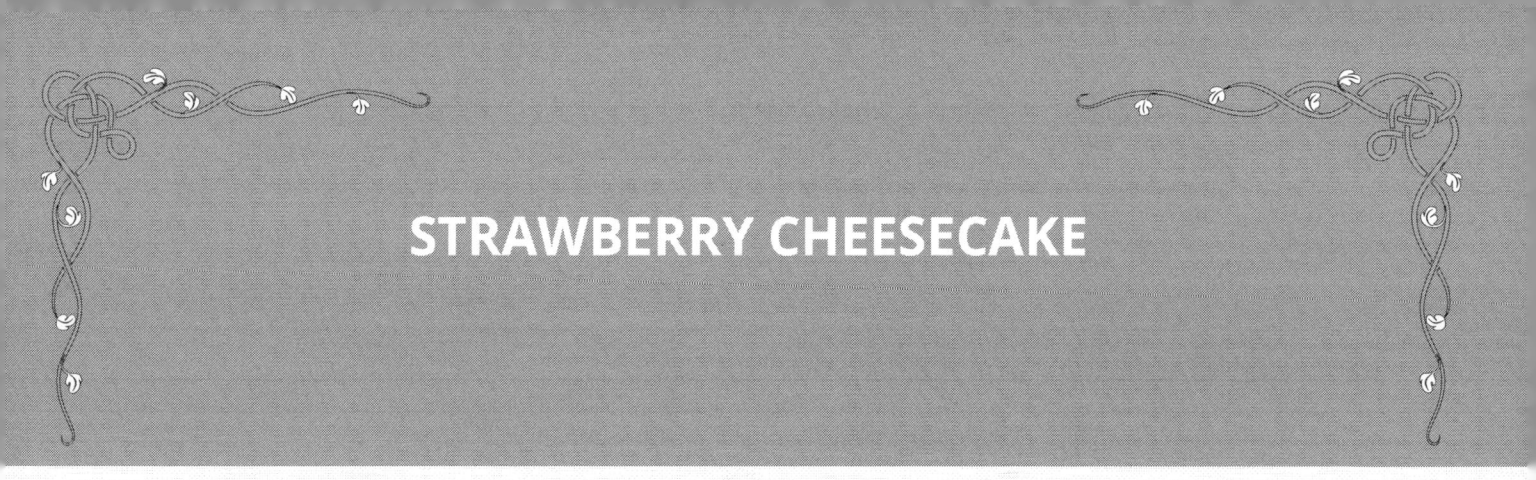

if you're looking to be health conscious without sacrificing flavor - go ahead and replace heavy cream cheese and sour cream with low fat versions plus Greek yogurt instead. For a crunchier crust, try lightly toasting the gluten-free cookies before crushing them. Remember to let the cheesecake cool completely before taking off that edge!

ALMOND AND ORANGE CAKE

Prep time: 15 minutes

Cooking Time: 40 minutes

Servings: 8

INGREDIENTS:

- 2 whole oranges
- 3 cups of almond flour
- 1 cup of sugar
- 1 teaspoon of gluten-free baking powder
- 1/2 teaspoon of salt
- 4 large eggs
- 1 teaspoon of vanilla extract

NUTRITIONS:

Calories: 280, Fats: 14g, Carbohydrates: 36g, Proteins: 6g, Fiber: 4g, Sugars: 18g

TIPS:

to take it to the next level try serving with a sprinkle of powdered sugar or dollop of freshly whipped cream. If you prefer something sweeter, feel free to give your batter an extra spoonful of sugar before baking. Make sure that when preparing the oranges they are cooked through thoroughly so that your cake has just the right texture.

DIRECTIONS:

1. Preheat the oven to 350 degrees F (175 degrees C). Grease a 9-inch cake pan.
2. Put the whole oranges in a pot and cover them with water. Bring to a boil and cook for 30 minutes, then drain and let cool. Once cooled, cut the oranges in half, remove the seeds, and finely chop in a food processor.
3. In a large bowl, mix the almond flour, sugar, baking powder, and salt. In another bowl, beat the eggs with the vanilla extract, then add the chopped oranges. Add the egg and orange mixture to the dry ingredients and mix until you get a homogeneous dough.
4. Pour the dough into the prepared pan and level the surface with a spatula.
5. Bake in the preheated oven for 40 minutes, or until a toothpick inserted in the center comes out clean. Let cool in the pan for 10 minutes, then transfer to a rack to cool completely.

OATMEAL AND CRANBERRY COOKIES

Prep time: 15 minutes

Cooking Time: 15 minutes

Servings: 12

INGREDIENTS:

- 2 cups of gluten-free oat flakes
- 1 cup of almond flour
- 1/2 cup of dried cranberries
- 1/2 cup of pure maple syrup
- 1/2 cup of coconut oil, melted
- 1 teaspoon of vanilla extract
- 1/2 teaspoon of cinnamon
- 1/4 teaspoon of salt

DIRECTIONS:

1. Preheat the oven to 350 degrees F (175 degrees C). Line a baking sheet with parchment paper.
2. In a large bowl, mix the oat flakes, almond flour, cranberries, maple syrup, coconut oil, vanilla extract, cinnamon, and salt until you get a homogeneous dough.
3. Use a spoon to gather the dough and form cookies on the prepared baking sheet.
4. Bake in the preheated oven for 15 minutes, or until the cookies are golden. Let cool on the baking sheet for 5 minutes, then transfer to a rack to cool completely.

NUTRITIONS:

Calories: 180, Fats: 9g, Carbohydrates: 20g, Proteins: 4g, Fiber: 3g, Sugars: 10g

TIPS:

For some variation in flavor and texture in these cookies, substitute cranberries with other dried fruits. To make them even more indulgent - why not drizzle over some maple syrup?

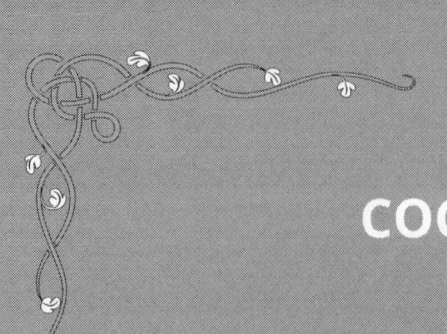

COCONUT AND MANGO CHIA PUDDING

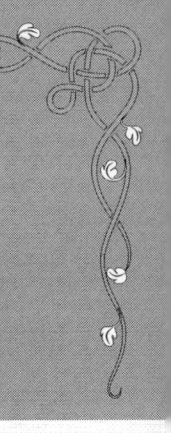

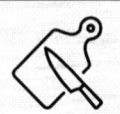

Prep time: 10 minutes

Cooking Time: 4 hours

Servings: 4

INGREDIENTS:

- 1/4 cup of chia seeds
- 1 cup of coconut milk
- 1 tablespoon of pure maple syrup
- 1 teaspoon of vanilla extract
- 1 ripe mango, peeled and cut into cubes

DIRECTIONS:

1. In a medium bowl, mix the chia seeds, coconut milk, maple syrup, and vanilla extract. Let it rest for 5 minutes, then stir again to prevent the chia seeds from clumping.
2. Cover the bowl and put it in the refrigerator for at least 4 hours, or until the pudding has reached the desired consistency.
3. Before serving, garnish with the mango cubes.

NUTRITIONS:

Calories: 200, Fats: 10g, Carbohydrates: 25g, Proteins: 5g, Fiber: 8g, Sugars: 12g

TIPS:

swap out mangoes for whatever fruit tickles your fancy from strawberries to kiwis – get creative! As a final flourish top off each glass with some gluten-free granola. Don't forget one important step - stir up that chia seed mixture after five minutes rest time otherwise those pesky little seeds will clump together resulting in lumpy pudding.

BANANA AND PEANUT BUTTER ICE CREAM

Prep time: 10 minutes

Cooking Time: 4 hours

Servings: 4

INGREDIENTS:

- 4 ripe bananas, cut into slices and frozen
- 2 tablespoons of natural peanut butter
- 1/2 teaspoon of vanilla extract
- A pinch of salt
- Gluten-free dark chocolate flakes, for garnish (optional)

DIRECTIONS:

1. Put the frozen bananas, peanut butter, vanilla extract, and salt in a food processor. Blend until you get a smooth and creamy consistency.
2. You can serve the ice cream immediately for a softer consistency, or you can transfer it to a container and put it in the freezer for at least 4 hours for a firmer consistency.
3. Before serving, garnish with the dark chocolate flakes, if desired.

NUTRITIONS:

Calories: 210, Fats: 8g, Carbohydrates: 35g, Proteins: 5g, Fiber: 4g, Sugars: 18g

TIPS:

Make sure you use ripe bananas to make this ice cream, as they will bring out a naturally sweet flavor. If you're not into peanut butter, feel free to switch it up with your favorite nut butter. To give it an extra kick of sweetness, try adding some maple syrup or honey. The texture of the finished product can vary depending on how long you freeze it for so don't be afraid to experiment until you get the perfect consistency that's truly 'you'.

Bread, Pasta & Pizza

OLIVE OIL AND ROSEMARY BREAD

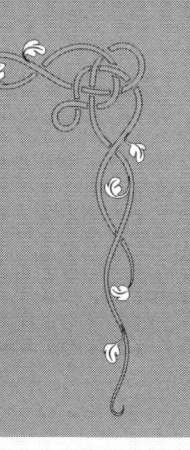

Prep time: 15 minutes

Cooking Time: 40 minutes

Servings: 1 loaf

INGREDIENTS:

- 1 cup of rice flour
- 1/2 cup of tapioca flour
- 1/2 cup of almond flour
- 1 packet of active dry yeast
- 1 teaspoon of salt
- 1 teaspoon of sugar
- 2 teaspoons of xanthan gum
- 1 cup of warm water
- 2 tablespoons of extra virgin olive oil
- 2 tablespoons of chopped fresh rosemary

NUTRITIONS:

Calories: 120, Fats: 2g, Carbohydrates: 22g, Proteins: 3g, Fiber: 2g, Sugars: 1g.

DIRECTIONS:

1. In a large bowl, mix together the flours, yeast, salt, sugar, and xanthan gum.
2. Add the warm water and olive oil to the flour mixture. Work the dough until it is smooth.
3. Add the chopped rosemary to the dough and mix until it is evenly distributed.
4. Cover the bowl with a damp cloth and let the dough rise in a warm place for about 1 hour, or until the dough has doubled in volume.
5. Preheat the oven to 375 degrees Fahrenheit (190 degrees Celsius).
6. Transfer the dough to a baking pan lined with parchment paper and bake in the preheated oven for about 40 minutes, or until the bread is golden and sounds hollow when tapped on the bottom.
7. Let the bread cool on the rack before slicing it.

TIPS:

When prepping the dough it's essential to mix all dry ingredients together before adding any liquids; this helps distribute yeast and xanthan gum evenly – ensuring perfect rising and texture. Don't wanna bother with making your own flour blend? Store bought gluten-free mixes usually have xanthan gum already included so no need to worry.

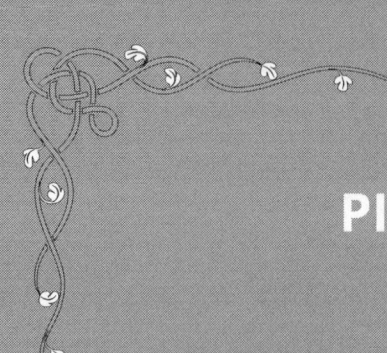

PIZZA WITH MOZZARELLA AND TOMATOES

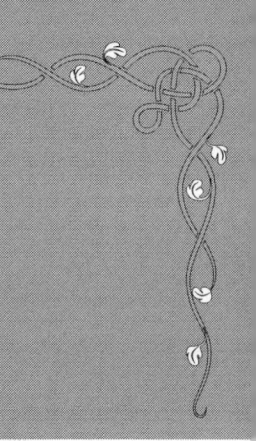

Prep time: 30 minutes

Cooking Time: 15 minutes

Servings: 2 pizza

INGREDIENTS:

- 1/2 cup of rice flour
- 1/2 cup of tapioca flour
- 1/2 cup of amaranth flour
- 1/2 cup of potato starch
- 2 teaspoons of xanthan gum
- 1 packet of active dry yeast
- 1 teaspoon of salt
- 1 cup of warm water (add gradually and adjust based on the consistency of the dough)
- 2 tablespoons of extra virgin olive oil
- 1 cup of tomato sauce
- 2 cups of shredded mozzarella
- 2 ripe tomatoes, sliced
- Fresh basil leaves for garnish

NUTRITIONS:

Calories: 600, Fats: 20g, Carbohydrates: 80g, Proteins: 25g, Fiber: 5g, Sugars: 8g.

TIPS:

For a truly scrumptious focaccia, it's all about the dough. When preparing your gluten-free mix, make sure to blend together the dry ingredients well before adding any liquids. This will ensure an even distribution of yeast and xanthan gum for optimal fluffiness and texture when cooked. If you opt for a pre-made flour mix then you won't need to worry about incorporating potato starch or xanthan gum at all!

DIRECTIONS:

1. In a large bowl, mix together the flours, potato starch, yeast, salt, and xanthan gum.
2. Add the warm water and 1 tablespoon of olive oil to the flour mixture. Work the dough until it is smooth.
3. Cover the bowl with a damp cloth and let the dough rise in a warm place for about 1 hour, or until the dough has doubled in volume.
4. Preheat the oven to 475 degrees Fahrenheit (245 degrees Celsius).
5. Divide the dough into two equal parts and roll out each part on a baking pan lined with parchment paper.
6. Spread the tomato sauce evenly on each pizza base.
7. Sprinkle the shredded mozzarella over the tomato sauce.
8. Arrange the tomato slices on the mozzarella.
9. Bake the pizzas in the preheated oven for about 15 minutes, or until the crust isgolden and the cheese is bubbling and slightly golden.
10. Garnish the cooked pizzas with fresh basil leaves before serving.

ROSEMARY AND COARSE SALT FOCACCIA

Prep time: 20 minutes

Cooking Time: 20 minutes

Servings: 8

INGREDIENTS:

- 1 cup of rice flour
- 1/2 cup of tapioca flour
- 1/2 cup of potato starch
- 2 teaspoons of xanthan gum
- 1 packet of active dry yeast
- 1 teaspoon of salt
- 1 cup of warm water (add gradually and adjust based on the consistency of the dough)
- 2 tablespoons of extra virgin olive oil
- 1 tablespoon of chopped fresh rosemary
- Coarse salt for garnish

NUTRITIONS:

Calories: 180, Fats: 4g, Carbohydrates: 32g, Proteins: 3g, Fiber: 2g, Sugars: 1g.

TIPS:

For extra flavor, why not add in to the dough some chopped garlic or onion powder - just don't overwork it as this can result in a denser end product.

DIRECTIONS:

1. In a large bowl, mix together the flours, potato starch, yeast, salt, and xanthan gum.
2. Add the warm water and 1 tablespoon of olive oil to the flour mixture. Work the dough until it is smooth.
3. Cover the bowl with a damp cloth and let the dough rise in a warm place for about 1 hour, or until the dough has doubled in volume.
4. Preheat the oven to 400 degrees Fahrenheit (200 degrees Celsius).
5. Roll out the dough on a baking pan lined with parchment paper. Create small dimples on the surface of the dough with your fingers.
6. Brush the dough with the remaining olive oil, sprinkle with the chopped rosemary and coarse salt.
7. Bake the focaccia in the preheated oven for about 20 minutes, or until it is golden.

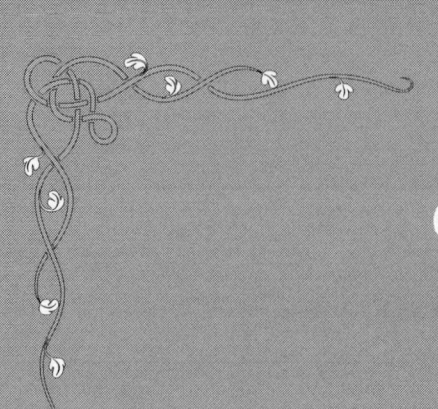

GLUTEN-FREE GNOCCHI

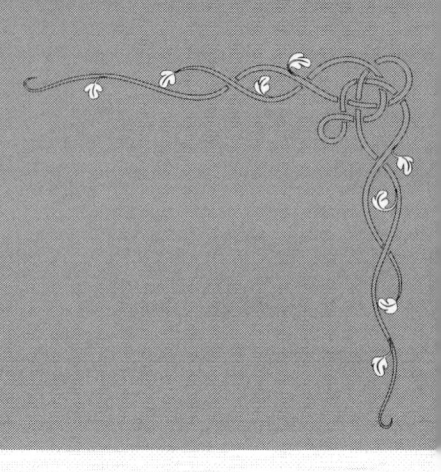

Prep time: 40 minutes

Cooking Time: 2-3 minutes

Servings: 4

INGREDIENTS:

- 2 large potatoes
- 1 cup of rice flour
- 1/2 teaspoon of salt
- 1 large egg

DIRECTIONS:

1. Cook the potatoes in a pot of boiling water until they are tender. Drain and let cool.
2. Once cooled, peel them and pass them through a potato masher into a large bowl.
3. Add the rice flour and salt to the mashed potatoes and mix until they are well combined.
4. Make a well in the center of the potato and flour mixture and break the egg into it.
5. Work the dough until it is smooth and well blended.
6. Divide the dough into smaller pieces and roll each one into a long "snake". Cut the snake into small pieces to form the gnocchi.
7. Cook the gnocchi in a pot of salted boiling water for 2-3 minutes, or until they float to the surface.

NUTRITIONS:

Calories: 220, Fats: 1g, Carbohydrates: 48g, Proteins: 5g, Fiber: 3g, Sugars: 1g.

TIPS:

When cooking up some gnocchi, sprinkle them with rice flour beforehand so they don't stick together during boiling; also try not to overcrowd the pot as that could damage their delicate structure (gluten-free ones especially!).

FRESH GLUTEN-FREE PASTA

Prep time: 30 minutes

Cooking Time: 30 minutes

Servings: 4

INGREDIENTS:

- 2 cups of rice flour
- 1/2 teaspoon of salt
- 2 large eggs
- Water, as needed

NUTRITIONS:

Calories: 300, Fats: 3g, Carbohydrates: 60g, Proteins: 7g, Fiber: 2g, Sugars: 0g.

DIRECTIONS:

1. In a large bowl, mix together the rice flour and salt.
2. Make a well in the center of the flour mixture and break the eggs into it.
3. Using a fork, start mixing the eggs, gradually incorporating the flour from the edge of the well.
4. Continue to work the dough, adding water a little at a time, until it is smooth and well blended. The dough should be elastic but not sticky. If it's too dry, add more water. If it's too wet, add a little more flour.
5. Cover the dough with a damp cloth and let it rest for 30 minutes.
6. After resting, roll out the dough on a floured surface to the desired thickness, then cut into your preferred pasta shape.

TIPS:

For best results, work quickly and evenly as this type of pasta tends to dry out faster than regular options. If it's too sticky on your work surface or rolling pin, add some extra rice flour – but be gentle when handling! Gradually incorporate water until the dough reaches the perfect consistency – don't forget that it's easier to add more liquid if needed than take away if there is too much! If you prefer you can either use a ready-made mix or create your own blend.

GLUTEN-FREE TAGLIATELLE

Prep time: 40 minutes

Cooking Time: 30 minutes

Servings: 4

INGREDIENTS:

- 2 cups of rice flour
- 1/2 teaspoon of salt
- 2 large eggs
- Water, as needed

NUTRITIONS:

Calories: 300, Fats: 3g, Carbohydrates: 60g, Proteins: 7g, Fiber: 2g, Sugars: 0g.

TIPS:

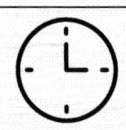

When prepping your gluten-free tagliatelle, it's important to roll out the dough evenly for uniform cooking. If it sticks to the work surface or rolling pin, sprinkle a bit more rice flour so you don't damage this delicate pasta.

DIRECTIONS:

1. In alarge bowl, mix together the rice flour and salt.
2. Make a well in the center of the flour mixture and break the eggs into it.
3. Using a fork, start mixing the eggs, gradually incorporating the flour from the edge of the well.
4. Continue to work the dough, adding water a little at a time, until it is smooth and well blended. The dough should be elastic but not sticky. If it's too dry, add more water. If it's too wet, add a little more flour.
5. Cover the dough with a damp cloth and let it rest for 30 minutes.
6. After resting, roll out the dough on a floured surface to about 1/8 inch thickness.
7. Using a pasta wheel or a sharp knife, cut the dough into long strips about 1/2 inch wide to create the tagliatelle.
8. Cook the tagliatelle in a pot of salted boiling water for 2-3 minutes, or until they are al dente.

WHOLE WHEAT BREAD

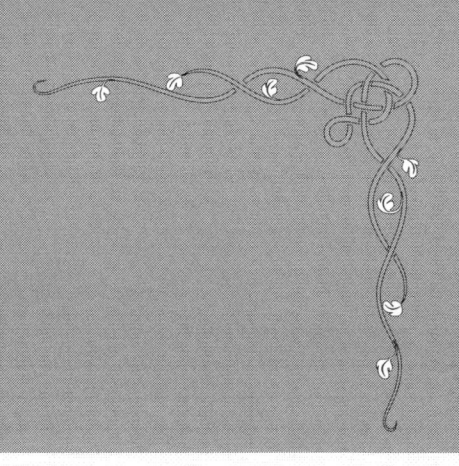

Prep time: 15 minutes

Cooking Time: 45 minutes

Servings: 1 loaf

INGREDIENTS:

- 1 cup of whole grain rice flour
- 1 cup of sorghum flour
- 1/2 cup of amaranth flour
- 1/2 cup of flaxseed flour
- 3 teaspoons of xanthan gum
- 1 packet of active dry yeast
- 1 teaspoon of salt
- 1 and 1/2 cup of warm water (add gradually and adjust based on the consistency of the dough)
- 2 tablespoons of extra virgin olive oil

NUTRITIONS:

Calories: 180, Fats: 3g, Carbohydrates: 35g, Proteins: 5g, Fiber: 5g, Sugars: 1g.

DIRECTIONS:

1. In a large bowl, mix together the flours, xanthan gum, yeast, and salt.
2. Make a well in the center of the flour mixture and add the warm water and olive oil.
3. Mix until the ingredients are well combined and the dough is smooth.
4. Cover the bowl with a damp cloth and let the dough rise in a warm place for about 1 hour, or until the dough has doubled in volume.
5. Preheat the oven to 375 degrees Fahrenheit (190 degrees Celsius).
6. Transfer the dough to a baking pan lined with parchment paper and bake in the preheated oven for about 45 minutes, or until the bread is golden and sounds hollow when tapped on the bottom.

TIPS:

For an ultra soft bread loaf with no hard crusts in sight, cover your baking pan with aluminum foil during the first 20-30 minutes of baking - just keep in mind that due to its texture, gluten-free bread may not rise as much as conventional recipes.

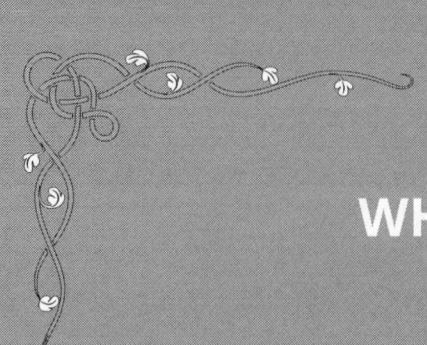

WHOLE WHEAT GLUTEN-FREE PIZZA

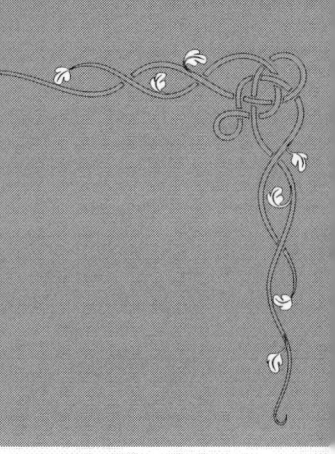

Prep time: 60 minutes

Cooking Time: 15-20 minutes

Servings: 2 medium pizza

INGREDIENTS:

- 2 cups of whole grain rice flour
- 1 cup of whole grain buckwheat flour
- 1/2 cup of tapioca flour
- 3 teaspoons of xanthan gum
- 1 teaspoon of salt
- 1 teaspoon of sugar
- 2 teaspoons of active dry yeast
- 1 and 1/4 cups of warm water (add gradually and adjust based on the consistency of the dough)
- 2 tablespoons of extra virgin olive oil
- for the topping:
- Tomato sauce
- Gluten-free cheese of choice
- Topping ingredients (mozzarella, tomatoes, mushrooms, etc.)

DIRECTIONS:

1. In a large bowl, mix together the whole grain rice, buckwheat, and tapioca flours.
2. Add the xanthan gum, salt, sugar, and active dry yeast. Mix the dry ingredients well.
3. Add the warm water and olive oil. Mix until you get a homogeneous dough.
4. Cover the bowl with a damp cloth and let the dough rise in a warm place for about 1 hour, or until it doubles in volume.
5. Preheat the oven to 220°C.
6. Divide the dough in half and roll out each half on a pizza pan lined with parchment paper.
7. Add the tomato sauce on the surface of the pizzas and distribute the cheese and the topping ingredients as you like.
8. Bake the pizzas in the preheated oven for 15-20 minutes, or until the crust is golden and crispy.
9. Remove the pizzas from the oven and let them cool slightly before cutting and serving.

NUTRITIONS:

Calories: 280, Fats: 7g, Carbohydrates: 48g, Proteins: 5g, Fiber: 3g, Sugars: 1g.

TIPS:

Spice it up with some aromatic herbs like oregano or rosemary! Make sure to let your dough rise in a warm spot free from any drafts, that way you'll be able to get the best leavening.

GLUTEN-FREE BREADSTICKS

Prep time: 20 minutes

Cooking Time: 20-25 minutes

Servings: about 20 breadsticks

INGREDIENTS:

- 1 and 1/2 cups of rice flour
- 1/2 cup of potato starch
- 1/4 cup of tapioca flour
- 2 teaspoons of xanthan gum
- 1 teaspoon of salt
- 1 teaspoon of sugar
- 1 teaspoon of active dry yeast
- 3/4 cup of warm water (add gradually and adjust based on the consistency of the dough)
- 3 tablespoons of extra virgin olive oil
- Sesame or poppy seeds for garnish (optional)

NUTRITIONS:

Calories: 100, Fats: 2g, Carbohydrates: 20g, Proteins: 1g, Fiber: 2g, Sugars: 1g.

TIPS:

Sprinkle a bit of rice flour onto your work surface and the dough for easier handling. If thin is more your style, roll out with a rolling pin and cut into strips. To get that ideal crispiness, lightly brush with olive oil before baking!

DIRECTIONS:

1. In a large bowl, mix together the rice flour, potato starch, tapioca flour, xanthan gum, salt, sugar, and active dry yeast.
2. Add the warm water and olive oil. Mix until you get a homogeneous dough.
3. Cover the bowl with a damp cloth and let the dough rest for about 15 minutes.
4. Preheat the oven to 180°C.
5. Divide the dough into small portions and shape each portion into a long, thin stick. You can do this by rolling the dough between your hands or on a lightly floured surface.
6. If you wish, you can sprinkle the breadsticks with sesame or poppy seeds for garnish, pressing them lightly onto the dough.
7. Transfer the breadsticks to a baking sheet lined with parchment paper, leaving enough space between them for leavening.
8. Bake the breadsticks in the preheated oven for 20-25 minutes, or until they are golden and crispy.
9. Remove the breadsticks from the oven and let them cool completely before serving.

GLUTEN-FREE RAVIOLI

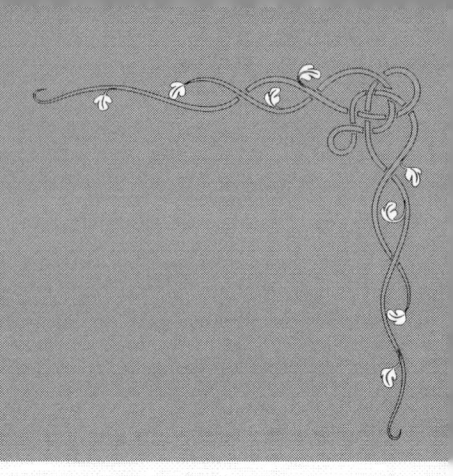

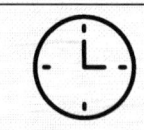

Prep time: 1 hour

Cooking Time: 10-12 minutes

Servings: 4-6

INGREDIENTS:

- 2 cups of gluten-free flour (you can use a mix of gluten-free flours such as rice flour, corn flour, potato starch, etc.)
- 1 teaspoon of xanthan gum
- 1 teaspoon of salt
- 3 large eggs
- 1-2 tablespoons of water (if necessary)
- for the filling:
- 7/8 cup of gluten-free ricotta
- 2/3 cup of fresh spinach, boiled and squeezed
- ½ cup of grated gluten-free cheese (like Parmigiano Reggiano or Pecorino Romano)
- Salt and pepper to taste

NUTRITIONS:

Calories: 275, Fats: 9g, Carbohydrates: 37g, Proteins: 12g, Fiber: 3g, Sugars: 1g.

TIPS:

Make sure that your seal is tight – no one wants any of the tasty filling spilling out during cooking! To store for later, arrange them on a baking tray lined with parchment paper and freeze before transferring into an airtight container. When it's time to eat, these can be cooked straight from frozen without defrosting - just add a couple extra minutes onto the cooking time.

DIRECTIONS:

1. In a large bowl, mix the gluten-free flour, xanthan gum, and salt.
2. Add the eggs and mix with a fork or your hands until you get a homogeneous dough. If necessary, add a little water to make the dough soft but not sticky.
3. Transfer the dough to a lightly floured surface and work it for a few minutes until it becomes smooth and elastic.
4. Wrap the dough in cling film and let it rest in the refrigerator for at least 30 minutes.
5. In the meantime, prepare the filling by mixing together the ricotta, boiled and squeezed spinach, grated gluten-free cheese, salt, and pepper. Taste the filling and adjust the salt and pepper according to your taste.
6. Divide the dough into two parts and work one part at a time.
7. Roll out the dough with a rolling pin or a pasta machine until you get a thin sheet.
8. With the help of a round glass or a pasta cutter, cut out circles of pasta from the sheet.
9. Put a teaspoon of filling in the center of each pasta circle.
10. Fold the pasta circle in half, sealing the edges well with your fingers or a fork. Make sure there are no air bubbles inside the ravioli.
11. Repeat the process with the rest of the dough and filling.
12. Bring a pot of salted water to a boil and cook the ravioli for 10-12 minutes, or until they are al dente.
13. Drain the ravioli gently and season them with the desired condiment, such as tomato sauce, melted butter and sage, or pesto.
14. Serve the ravioli hot and garnish them with grated gluten-free cheese, fresh aromatic herbs, or a sprinkle of pepper.

RUSTIC GLUTEN-FREE PIZZA

Prep time: 1 hour

Cooking Time: 20-25 minutes

Servings: 4-6

INGREDIENTS:

- 1 cup of rice flour
- 1/2 cup of corn flour
- 1/2 cup of potato starch
- 1 teaspoon of xanthan gum
- 1 teaspoon of salt
- 1 teaspoon of sugar
- 1 teaspoon of active dry yeast
- 1 and 1/2 cup of warmwater (add gradually and adjust based on the consistency of the dough)
- 2 tablespoons of extra virgin olive oil
- for the topping:
- 1 cup of tomato sauce
- 7/8 cup of gluten-free salami, cut into thin slices
- 7/8 cup of gluten-free cheese slices (like mozzarella or provolone)
- 1/2 cup of black olives, pitted and sliced
- 1 teaspoon of dried oregano
- Red pepper flakes (optional)
- Salt and pepper to taste

NUTRITIONS:

Calories: 370, Fats: 13g, Carbohydrates: 48g, Proteins: 13g, Fiber: 4g, Sugars: 4g.

TIPS:

try rolling out the gluten-free dough thinner than usual if you prefer thin bases. The rustic gluten-free pizza can be stored in the refrigerator and reheated in the oven before serving.

DIRECTIONS:

1. In a large bowl, mix the gluten-free flour, xanthan gum, salt, sugar, and active dry yeast.
2. Add the warm water and olive oil. Mix until you get a homogeneous dough.
3. Cover the bowl with a damp cloth and let the dough rise in a warm place for about 1 hour, or until it doubles in volume.
4. Preheat the oven to 220°C (428°F).
5. Transfer the dough to a lightly floured surface and briefly work it to deflate it.
6. Divide the dough in half and roll out each half on a pizza tray lined with baking paper, giving them a round or rectangular shape.
7. Spread the tomato sauce evenly on the surface of the pizzas.
8. Arrange the salami slices on the tomato sauce, followed by the cheese slices and sliced olives. Add the oregano, red pepper flakes (if desired), and season with salt and pepper to taste.
9. Bake the pizzas in the preheated oven for 20-25 minutes, or until the crust is golden and crispy and the cheese is melted and slightly golden.
10. Remove the pizzas from the oven and let them cool slightly before cutting and serving them.

CONCLUSION

As we wrap up this voyage through the world of gluten-free living, we hope you've found this book to be much more than a cookbook. It's an inspiration, your companion and friend on your sometimes challenging yet always rewarding journey into the realm of life without gluten.

We've not only supplied recipes but also tips & tricks, personal experiences and practical advice that will help you stay positive throughout it all. We want to be like that one person who keeps cheering for you - encouragingly pushing forward while never forgetting why it's important to take care of yourself in every way possible.

It isn't about depriving yourself; rather it is about discovering new flavors and ingredients while establishing healthy habits so as to live better each day! Embrace change with open arms today by making use of what works best for YOU!

Cheers to your gluten-free journey! May it be filled with flavorful meals, unforgettable memories and a sense of accomplishment for taking the best care you can of yourself and those around you. Every step is a leap towards improved health and an enhanced life so keep setting goals - no matter how small - that will help make this lifestyle change easier.

We are excited to join in on your delicious experience! If our book was beneficial to you, we would greatly appreciate if took the time outto write us an honest review on Amazon. This feedback will allow us to continuously improve plus helps others discover what we offer too; because here's one thing worth celebrating: Your wellbeing.

APPENDIX 1

Measurement Conversions

Volume Equivalents (Liquid)

US STANDARD	US STANDARD (OUNCES)	METRIC (APPROXIMATE)
2 tablespoons	1 fl. oz.	30 mL
1/4 cup	2 fl. oz.	60 mL
1/2 cup	4 fl. oz.	120 mL
1 cup	8 fl. oz.	240 mL
1 1/2 cups	12 fl. oz.	355 mL
2 cups or 1 pint	16 fl. oz.	475 mL
4 cups or 1 quart	32 fl. oz.	1 L
1 gallon	128 fl. oz.	4 L

Volume Equivalents (Dry)

US STANDARD	METRIC (APPROXIMATE)
1/8 teaspoon	0.5 mL
1/4 teaspoon	1 mL
1/2 teaspoon	2 mL
3/4 teaspoon	4 mL
1 teaspoon	5 mL
1 tablespoon	15 mL
1/4 cup	59 mL
1/3 cup	79 mL
1/2 cup	118 mL
2/3 cup	156 mL
3/4 cup	177 mL
1 cup	235 mL
2 cups or 1 pint	475 mL
3 cups	700 mL
4 cups or 1 quart	1 L

Oven Temperatures

FAHRENHEIT	CELSIUS (APPROXIMATE)
250°F	120°C
300°F	150°C
325°F	165°C
350°F	180°C
375°F	190°C
400°F	200°C
425°F	220°C
450°F	230°C

APPENDIX 2
Recipe Index

A

Almond and Orange Cake, 90
Apple Cake, 80
Avocado Toast, 27

B

Baked Kale Chips, 69
Baked Salmon with Honey Mustard Sauce, 51
Baked Zucchini Chips, 77
Banana and Peanut Butter Ice Cream, 93
Banana and Strawberry Smoothie, 23
Banana and Walnut Muffins, 25
Banana Pancakes, 83
Beef Chili, 64
Beef Fajitas, 58
Beet Hummus, 67
Black Bean and Quinoa Salad, 34
Buckwheat and Roasted Vegetable Salad, 45

C

Carrot Cake, 84
Chicken and Zucchini Meatballs, 76
Chickpea and Spinach Curry, 59
Chocolate Brownies, 82
Chocolate Cookies, 81
Classic Sugar-Free Cookies, 87

Coconut and Berry Smoothie Bowl, 31
Coconut and Mango Chia Pudding, 92
Crispy Zucchini Sticks, 66
Curry Chicken with Basmati Rice, 47

F

Fresh Gluten-Free Pasta, 99
Fruit and Granola Yogurt, 28

G

Gluten-Free Breadsticks, 103
Gluten-Free Gnocchi, 98
Gluten-Free Ravioli, 104
Gluten-Free Tagliatelle, 100
Greek Chicken Salad, 43
Grilled Beef Steak with Roasted Vegetable Side, 63
Grilled Chicken and Avocado Sandwich, 36
Grilled Eggplant Rolls, 52
Grilled Fish Tacos, 39
Grilled Salmon with Lemon and Parsley Sauce, 62
Grilled Shrimp with Garlic Sauce, 55

H

Homemade Gluten-Free Granola, 26
Hunter's Chicken, 61

L

Lemon and Poppy Seed Muffins, 79
Lemon and Rosemary Chicken, 50
Lentil and Sausage Stew, 54
Lentil and Vegetable Soup, 37
Low-Sugar Chocolate Pudding, 86
Low-Sugar Pumpkin Muffins, 85

M

Mini Eggplant Pizzas, 68
Mushroom Risotto, 38

O

Oat Pancakes with Blueberries, 21
Oatmeal and Cranberry Cookies, 91
Olive Oil and Rosemary Bread, 95

P

Pizza with Mozzarella and Tomatoes, 96
Pork Steak with Apple Sauce, 53
Potato and Leek Soup, 35
Primavera Pasta, 41

Q

Quinoa and Apple Porridge, 24
Quinoa and Spinach Meatballs, 70
Quinoa with Grilled Vegetables, 46

R

Rosemary and Coarse Salt Focaccia, 97
Rustic Gluten-Free Pizza, 105

S

Scrambled Eggs with Vegetables and Cheese, 32
Shrimp and Pineapple Skewers, 75
Spinach and Feta Frittata, 22, 48
Spinach and Tomato Frittata, 42
Strawberry Cheesecake, 89
Sugar-Free Coconut Panna Cotta, 88
Sweet Potato and Red Pepper Soup, 57
Sweet Potato Crostini with Avocado and Smoked Salmon, 72
Sweet Potato Nachos, 74
Sweet Potato Pancakes, 30

T

Teriyaki Chicken, 56
Teriyaki Chicken with Rice, 40
Tomato and Basil Bruschetta, 71
Turkey and Quinoa Meatballs, 44

V

Vegan Buddha Bowl, 60
Vegetable Quiche, 29

W

Whole Wheat Bread, 101
Whole Wheat Gluten-Free Pizza, 102

Made in United States
Orlando, FL
17 December 2023